A POT AND
A WINDOW

A POT AND A WINDOW

*Family Stories of Challenge,
Triumph, and Other Reflections*

Howard D. Branch

A Pot and A Window
Family Stories of Challenge, Triumph, and Other Reflections

Howard D. Branch

First Edition

ISBN: 979-8-218-09000-5
Library of Congress Control Number: 2022948551

BLAF Press

To my siblings, living and deceased, and to our deceased parents that raised us to be respectful, kind and helpful to family, friends, strangers, and especially to our elders.

Acknowledgements

First and foremost, I must acknowledgement the role faith played in this undertaking. I have never attempted anything like this in the past. Additionally, a number of earthly individuals helped bring this publication to completion. Sisters, Susie and Lena, were my partners in crime once the manuscript began to take shape. Sister, Belinda, picked up the baton when a chapter was added late in the development. In addition to checking for the usual misspelling and grammatical errors, they made welcomed additions and deletions. Brother Frank was the repository for dates and other tidbits. Cathy Smith's virtual "Memoir Writing" class provided resources that proved invaluable in getting from manuscript to a finished product.

Contents

Introduction

For more than thirty-five years I have been threatening to write a book that sort of chronicles my growth and that of my siblings as we grew up in the Deep South. Our family's geographic center is in Coila (Carroll County), Mississippi. While our life and the lives of many of our cousins and friends form the basis of this mostly non-fiction work. It is not meant to be autobiographical; nor does this represent years of scholarly research. In fact, I worried that formal research might make the book too academic and less authentic. We captured the facts as we remembered them. No doubt other families or other individuals remember the same information slightly differently. Hopefully this book honors our parents, Will Lee Branch, Sr. and Susie Mae Lockhart-Fullilove-Branch. Will was known as Cooter by most folks. Susie was called Sue by some and Suzette by others. Surely, they are smiling down on us from heaven. All 15 siblings contributed to this effort, knowingly or unknowingly. As lead author, I lament the fact that I did not push hard enough to complete this effort before two siblings and a number of other relatives and friends passed. I wish we had worked faster and more diligently. Not intentional, but there is likely a male slant on some of the information. This book is intended to be a light-hearted look at financially challenged families living in rural communities during the mid 1900s. Though our family serve as the basis for the content, we believe it to be reasonably representative of other, especially African American, families of similar socioeconomic backgrounds within our geographical region and likely far beyond. The book loosely depicts the time period from when the eldest sibling/sister would have turned six years old to when the youngest would have completed high school. I believe that most of us have some clear memories of things once we started school. If the math is correct this period equates to the 35 years between 1947 and 1982. As a set of fifteen siblings, we have never been into Genealogy. Most of us never knew our maternal nor paternal grandparents. We did not ask a lot of questions about them nor was a lot of information volunteered about them. We regret those missed opportunities to learn about another generation of our family. We have since wondered out loud and had some questions answered. In all likelihood, we have, not-so-distant, blood relatives scattered throughout the United States and in distant lands.

CHAPTER ONE

Births

A substantial number of African American children raised in rural areas were born outside of the confines of a hospital. Even if the family could have afforded it, it was not permitted. Most African American babies of the period were delivered at home by midwives. At that time, a midwife was a lady in the general vicinity that through various means had acquired knowledge and skills related to delivering babies at home. So was the case for me and my siblings. As the time for the baby to be born was imminent, someone would go get 'big mama' (midwife). A lucky few people actually had motorized transportation early on. While someone went for big mama, someone began to boil lots of water and gather clean towels. When the midwife arrived, all of the children and the husband were sent out of the room with great anticipation until the baby had been delivered.

During those early years, breast feeding was the norm. Otherwise, cow's milk was available along with store-bought brands. Then there was the powdered milk that came as part of the 'po' folk free food program.

In our world, there were no such things as pacifiers, walkers, strollers, infant swings, car seats and the like for us. You could not find baby foods, processed juices, nor disposable diaper at our house. You might say we were raised on the original organic food.

Our mother gave birth to 16 babies. Two of them were not long for this world. The second oldest child died weeks after birth. One child, of a set of twins, died at birth.

During this time, most male children were circumcised. This was one of many things that was done and generally accepted. No grownup ever said and 'this is why it was done'. Yes, we read what it said in the bible but that did not speak to us as non-Jewish people. It did not come up in the high school biology class. I dare say we only addressed the subject when we had our own male child(ren). For some the tradition was continued because that's the way it was done, for other perhaps religion entered the picture, and finally, there was hygiene considerations. Eventually the practice pretty much ceased.

For the longest, births on television were celebrated with the father handing out cigars. That did not happen in our community. Our father never handed out cigars, cigarettes or anything else of the sort. Presumably we were too cash strapped to afford such extravagance.

More than half of our siblings were named after a relative; uncle, aunt, grandparent, or a cousin. Perhaps with the exception of grandparents, we eventually met and came to know the individual we were named after. For example, our mother had a brother named Howard. She and both of her brothers named one of their sons Howard (yours truly). Often a child (not necessarily babies) would be given a nickname that often followed them into adulthood. There was little rhyme or reason behind the nicknames. Not everyone felt inclined to refer to the person by the nickname. Boot, Shoe, Put, Sang, Mookie and Cooter are some of the nicknames that readily come to mind. Interestingly, only a couple of us siblings had a nickname. Even to this day, some family and friends try to pen the moniker "Little Cooter" or "Little Coot" to one or more of the Branch boys, as Cooter was our father's nickname.

CHAPTER TWO

Employment/Work

W hen a teacher would ask 'what does your father do', we would reply that 'he is a farmer'. Implicit in the question, was the assumption that our mother did not work outside of the home. During those years, that was more likely than not to be true. To us there were only two categories of work, farming or 'public work', and our father was a farmer. Farm or farming were well known terms. Public work simply meant that the individual left home and went to a job, presumably in a factory or elsewhere such that the pay amount and pay interval were well understood. In our case, our father was not only a farmer but he fit the category of a sharecropper. At some point he moved into public work as it was, but as a family we did both. Even those individuals that went to an employer/employee job, typically did work back on the farm in the evenings and on the weekends. As years passed, males went off to a variety of jobs. Many worked for the Department of Agriculture planting seedlings (mostly pine trees) and some worked at the cotton gin. A number of men and women worked at three well-known factories in the area: a factory that made picture frames; one that manufactured pianos; and, one that did metal work. Of course, there were the bus drivers, many of whom that worked back on the farm between morning drop-offs at, and afternoon pickups from, school. The segregated elementary school had a staff of black female teachers and a black male principal. This also applied to the middle school but not high school. In our community, the church's pastors were exclusively black males. Then there were the one-off scenarios where black males worked as attendants at service stations (or "filling stations" as we called them) and as a helper in a grocery store. A number of young men joined the military. Progress was slow but steady. Eventually more males and females were able to attend college or trade schools. Even the farmers were able to improve their station in life as they acquired equipment that made their work less labor intensive and allowed them to expand the amount of land they farmed. This made the children's life easier also, including missing fewer days of school.

Logging

Logging was one of those jobs that did not require a formal education and a person could be his own boss.

It would often have operations that were upscale, and competing operations that were less complex, simply hoping to turn a buck. True logging by definition leaned in the upscale direction. An upstart operation was generally more of a pulp wood activity. The former required serious equipment, the latter could be started with a chainsaw. Cutting pulp wood was not for the faint of heart. While there was plenty of trees to cut, getting the wood to market (saw mill) required at least some minimum investment. Almost any truck larger than the typical pickup truck could be re-engineered to haul pulp wood. To get started in business, the truck could be loaded by hand. Eventually a winch would likely be added to replace the manual lifting. For the uninitiated, pulp wood would be cut to roughly 6 feet in length and loaded across the truck parallel to the cab. Logs on the other hand, would essentially be the full length of the cut tree and loaded length-wide on the truck that was essentially a semi-tractor-trailer.

Barbering

The males in our household would likely be grown and away from home before getting their hair cut by a professionally trained and licensed barber. At some point the older brothers were able to do a sufficient job at cutting hair. One of them eventually worked in a barber shop and had his own country barber shop of sort. Not surprisingly, several brothers picked up the trade, albeit not professionally. We did not think about it at the time but we were budding entrepreneurs. Initially, we used manual, none electric clippers. We would cut hair on the front porch when the weather permitted, inside the house at other times. We used single and double edge razor blades without the holder to outline the haircuts. We actually got pretty good at it. The better trained brother graduated to using a "straight razor". When we needed to have the clipper blades sharpened, we would put a one-dollar bill with the set of blades and wrap them in brown paper from a paper bag and send them through the mail to a shop several cities away. In a few days the sharpened blades would be returned to us. The cash money nor the blades were ever lost in shipment. The advancement to electric clippers made the job so much easier.

Other Jobs

Usually without any formal training, a person might figuratively or literally hang out their shingle as a carpenter, auto mechanic, barber, etc. Such a person might affectionately be referred to as a "jackleg" or "shade tree" this or that. For example, a "jackleg carpenter", or a "shade-tree mechanic". The "shade-tree mechanic" usually did not have an actual shop so he often worked on vehicles underneath a tree, for shade and attaching a pulley or hoist. There was nothing they couldn't fix with a clothes hanger, a pair pliers, and an adjustable wrench. The adjustable or crescent wrench was also known as a knuckle-buster as it was prone to slip when trying to remove a nut or bolt that was screwed on tight. That slippage often led to minor hand injuries, especially injuries to the knuckles.

CHAPTER THREE

Life on the Farm

Farming or living on the farm required waking up early, often before daylight. Parents may have relied on the crowing of the rooster, an alarm clock, or just the natural rhythm of their sleep/wake cycle. Awake or not, children did not move until they were called by a parent. There were a number of chores to be completed before getting to the ultimate efforts of a typical day; working in the field. Chores would range from feeding chickens, feeding hogs, bringing fire wood into the house, fetching water, etc. At times we had to search for and wrangler with the horses and mules in order to bring them home to support plowing and other efforts. All of these chores were likely completed before breakfast. The primary activities on the farm related to getting one or more crops planted, cultivated, and harvested; what some might refer to as the "money crops". Cotton was king and corn may have been the queen for the average farmer. Families with a sufficient amount of land would supplement the primary crops with sugar cane, or perhaps water melons. Other items were grown as much for eating as for selling; items such as white (Irish or ice) potato, sweet potato, and peanuts. In the springtime the soil would be prepared for planting. That involved a number of pieces of equipment, for example, a disc, a section harrow, and various plows. Using the middle buster plow was the chore from hell. Once the soil had been prepared, then came the actual planting. After planting came the cultivating. The soil prep, the planting, and the cultivating of the soil was done using equipment that was pulled by one or more mules or horses adorned with gear made of chains, leather, and wooden pieces. The bridle was always the first piece of gear for the animal. Depending on what piece of equipment was being used, one person would labor with the equipment (say a plow) and a second person would hold the line used to steer the individual or team of mules. The animals would relieve themselves when the mood hit them, often without stopping. So, one had to be mindful to avoid stepping into freshly minted equine urine or feces or both. Once the ground was sufficiently prepared, the crop of choice would be planted. After planting, the crop likely needed to be thinned out so that the remaining plants would have sufficient space to grow. The thinning would be done by individuals using a hoe or rake while also removing unwanted grass and weeds. The weeding would be repeated as needed. Commercial fertilizer and insecticide would typically be applied at least once during the growing season. After months of growth, the crops would be ready for harvesting. We harvested our crops by hand, for example, picking cotton. We often worked (always grudgingly) from sun up to sun down; particularly when picking cotton. If the harvest season was particularly rainy, we might end up picking cotton over into the winter; man, it would be cold in the field! At least once, we recall picking cotton into the new year in that we were not able to finish gathering it during the year in which it was planted.

Cotton would be taken to the gin for processing and payment would be received. Some corn would be harvested for eating while the stalks were still green. The rest would remain in the field and would be harvested when the corn ears and stalks were dry. This dry corn would be used as feed for livestock and for seed-corn for the next planting season. Some of the corn, like cotton, might be sold for income. As a sharecropper, revenue from the sale of the crops had to be split with the landowner. This often left the sharecropper with little or nothing to show for his efforts for that farming cycle.

Farm equipment

The larger pieces of equipment were the kind used in the field to cultivate the soil, to plant, etc. Equipment pulled by animals (such as horses, mules, or both) had one or more versions made to be pulled by a tractor as well. The method of use was not interchangeable. The equipment had names like a disc, distributor, insecticide sprayer, section harrow, and various plows. Many smaller pieces of farm equipment required only human power; equipment such as the hoe, rake, axe, sling blade, and Kaiser blade.

We had to construct a number of barbwire fences designed to restrict the travel of the animals and vehicles. The equipment needed would likely include a posthole digger, a crowbar, a claw hammer, nails, and barb wire. Occasionally, a "cattle-gap" might be constructed to keep livestock in or out of a particular area while allowing for vehicles to come and go without anyone having to get out of the vehicle to open and close a gate. Think of putting a bridge across a mote. However, the bridge is constructed with gaps in the 'floor' (perpendicular to the vehicle's travel) such that animals fear to tread.

Generally, wood would be cut using a single or double-bladed axe or a cross-cut saw. This included cutting the trees down then cutting them into manageable size pieces. The cross-cut saw had to be used by two individuals working in rhythm with each other. The wood was used in the stove to cook and in5 the heaters and fireplace to keep warm. A sledge hammer and a wedge might be used to split large diameter pieces into smaller pieces. The single bladed axe could be used instead of the wedge as it resembled a wedge attached to a wooden handle. Those same mules used to plow, would be used to pull a chained log from the woods to home so that it would be cut into approximately two feet long pieces of fire wood or perhaps into longer fence posts.

OTHER CHORES

Feeding Animals

Mules, horses, cows, hogs, chickens, all had to be fed each and every day. The larger animal (mules, horses, cows) would be allowed to graze in the pasture and would have to be fed only if they were kept in a pen. The type of feed would vary. Pretty much all animals would be fed corn at some point. Hogs were kept in a pen and therefore had to be fed daily. They might be given some corn or some finely grounded grain mixed with water. Often what was fed to the hogs was referred to as "slop"; therefore, the act of feeding the hogs was "slopping the hogs". The word slop would sometime be used to refer to food for human consumption, if the food was soupy and/ or did not smell inviting. The intended recipient of the food might say "I wouldn't feed that slop to my hogs". Of course, those could be fighting words.

Many farmers had cows. Cows could be sold for income, they could be a source of meat, and a source of milk. Milking the cows would be a chore. Sometimes they would be less than cooperative. Only the cows that had recently given birth would be milked as they were lactating. For some reason, only the eldest siblings had the favor of milking the cows. The milk might be given to babies, drank, used in cooking, and churned. Butter would be obtained from the churning process. Some of the whole milk would be converted into buttermilk, which also would also be drank and used in cooking.

Washing clothes

For the bulk of our childhood we did not have a washing machine. We washed clothes by hand in a number three (#3) round galvanized tub using a rub/wash board. Often the detergent would be lye soap. After ringing out the clothes by hand, we would then rinse them in a second tub of water, ring them out by hand and hang them on a clothesline out doors to dry in the air and sunshine. Some pieces required at least two individuals in order to fully ring out the water. The wooden clothes pen would be used to keep the clothes from blowing off the line due to a breeze or a gust of wind. Some heavy, and heavily soiled clothing like coverall would be boiled in a big outdoor pot. We eventually got a washing machine with the ringer. The ringer would often grab the hand of the uninitiated until he or she got used to it. We never got to the point of owning a dryer. A liquid referred to as "Bluing" would sometime be added to the rinse water for coveralls and jeans in order to freshen up the blueness.

Washing dishes

Washing dishes was usually a chore for the girls in the house; though boys were not totally off the hook.

The dishes were washed in a big pan filled with warm water. There would be a second pan of water for rinsing. Glasses (often used jelly jars) were washed first. Dishes were typically dried after washing as opposed to letting them drain and air dry. Therefore, dishwashing was usually a two-person task; one person washed and the second person rinsed and dried the dishes.

Sunday Morning Contradiction

We generally understood the scripture about keeping the Sabbath holy. Therefore, we did not do any serious work on Sundays, unless absolutely necessary. Of course, the animals had to be fed every day. Interestingly enough we did the bulk of the house cleaning on Sunday morning. Presumably because the other six days were devoted to work outside of the house. Sweeping and mopping got done on Sunday mornings. We used up quite a few brooms on the mostly wooden floors. The broom that were purchased at the 'store' was in fact a straw broom, but we simply called it the broom. The true "straw broom" was made at home by going out into the pasture or similar place and collecting straw that grew wild and fashioning that straw (held together by seagrass string) into a broom. The broom fashioned at home was not as effective as the ones made and sold commercially but it was much more affordable.

The girls had to shampoo their hair Saturday night, press it Sunday morning, roll it on (homemade) rollers made from tobacco cans that was cut into strips and covered with pieces from a brown paper bags in order to have curls. The hair was naturally curly and some-time known as "kinky". To increase the length of the hair, females used a heated straightening comb. They also used a heated Marcella/curling irons to curl the hair. Hair grease in the red or the blue containers was added to the hair prior to straightening and curling to aid in the process and to give the hair gloss/shine. This at home beauty salon activity occasionally took place on Saturday evening or Sunday morning. Not surprising there were the occasional burns. The person who's hair was being pressed or curled might be burned directly with the hot irons or hot grease. They would shake it off and the process would continue. Pain is sometime part of the cost of looking beautiful.

CHAPTER FOUR

Food

O ur primary foods included home-grown chickens, hogs, and vegetables. Hogs were kept in a pen so that they would not run away and to prevent them from eating or otherwise damage the garden. Occasionally they would get out and we would have to go find them and drive them home, cussing them all the way. The female hogs are sows and the males are boars. Rings were put into the hog's nose to reduce the rooting they would do. Often the male hogs were castrated and the testicles were eaten. No one seem to remember what they tasted like; chicken we suppose. We killed hogs during late fall or early winter. Sometimes the hogs to be killed were put into a special pen, so as to clean them out, in preparation for killing. Hog killing day could be a long day depending on the number of hogs to be killed. An older person with experience would kill the hog by shooting it in the head at close range using a handgun and then cutting its throat. Water was heated to boiling outside in a big black pot. Once the hog was killed it would typically be placed in a fifty-gallon drum, the boiling water would be poured over the hog so as to prepare to remove the hair from the hog. This was done by hand to the degree possible. A knife would be used to remove any residual hair; much like shaving. Once the hair was removed, the hog would be hung up by its hind legs. The hog's inner parts would be removed, the head removed, and the remainder would be cut into sections. During the early days, the primary way of storing the hog meat was to salt it down in a wooden box as we did not have a freezer in which to store it. Very little of a hog was wasted. Intestine (Chitterling), liver, the head (including the brain), feet, tail, etc. all went to good use. A holiday delicacy was hog-head souse, also known as hog-head cheese. We would also help other folks kill their hogs. At times we would be given the lesser parts of the hog as a form of payment for our help. Of course, this was a reciprocal practice, that is, we share our meat with persons that assisted us with the killing of our hogs. Next in the meat hierarchy was poultry or chickens. They were fairly easy to grow and to prepare. The scalding hot water in preparation to remove the feathers was similar to the process of removing the hair from the hog. The chickens were killed by chopping off the head with an axe or ringing the head off. Neither process was for the squeamish. A mature child was allowed to do the chopping; however, the ringing was reserved for grownups as that required a special touch.

For many years we had a substantial garden. We grew the usual greens (collars, turnips, mustards, and cabbages), purple hull peas, pole beans, butter beans, snaps beans, corn, squash, cucumbers, peppers, tomatoes and the like. Items grown outside of the garden in a 'patch' included, white potatoes, sometime referred to as or pronounced as Irish or ice potatoes. Other patch items included sweet potatoes, peanuts, and watermelons. A few families grew sugar cane that was primarily used in the making of Molasses. Cane grew in a fashion similar to corn, except that in the case of cane the stalks were the end product. There was cane that had a green stalk and one that had a purple stalk. When the cane was harvested, it had to be run through a press or mill that squeezed the juice out of it. A neighbor/cousin had one such mill. The horsepower for the mill would be a mule or horse walking around the equipment in a continuous circle. The juice squeezed from the cane would be heated/cooked as part of the process of turning it into molasses. The solid waste was discarded. Some of it might be given to livestock as feed. The cane stalks grew in segments roughly six to eight inches long. A few stalks would be diverted to direct and immediate enjoyment. After being cut into individual segments, one would peel off the wood-like exterior and chew on the inside material, enjoying the chewing process, swallowing the juice, and spitting out the residual material. This was another one of the enjoyments of farm living. Too much enjoyment by human or animal would often lead to an upset stomach and diarrhea.

Canning

Canning was the answer if the family wanted fruits and vegetables to be available beyond the growing season. The vegetables we grew were available directly from the garden only a few months during the year. The family would 'can' both fruits and vegetables. When items were purchased in a glass jar, the jars were often saved for later canning activities. The famous Mason Jars and other jars would be purchased to be used specifically for canning. Vegetables (greens, beans, peas, etc.) were easier to can. Certain vegetables would be pickled (cucumbers, beets, peppers, etc). Chow-chow (or Cha-cha) was a combination of vegetables (cabbage, onion, pepper, and green tomato) used during the cooking process to enhance the flavor of vegetables or used like a condiment. It could be kind of spicy or sweet. Fruits (apples, peaches, pears, etc.) would typically be pealed and the seeds/core removed. The peals from the fruits could be used in the making of jellies and jams. The canning was led by grownups, while the children would gather the fruits and vegetables and remove the peel or hulls. Some families had enough fruit trees to 'qualify' as having an orchard. Others had a few randomly located fruit and nut trees. The most readily available nut trees were the pecan and black walnut. The black walnut was a therapy nut. It would either drive one crazy or provide serenity by keeping the eater focused and distracted from his/her troubles. Many berries grew wild, without human intervention. They grew on a bush of sort call briar. The much heralded muscadines and grapes grew on vines. Plums grew on bushes. These fruits were also candidates for jellies and jams, or just eating a hand full. Almost all fruits, canned or otherwise were candidates for making pies as well. Then there was the rare persimmon tree. The persimmon could be the size of a small apple but it looked more like a plum, particularly its color (a deep orange). The seeds were also similar to the plum, but the persimmon had several seeds in a single unit.

Free Food Program

Not quite like manna from heaven, but at some point, we received free 'non-perishable' food. Not sure about the official name of the food/program but we knew it as commodity food; commodity meat; commodity cheese, powdered milk, beans/peas, etc. We enjoyed the taste of most of the items. The white beans and yellow split peas were not so inviting. The shredded chicken and shredded beef came in cans and were a bit more to our liking. The peanut butter was good but we eventually grew tired of it. We didn't like the idea of being in need; however, we appreciated the food. As kids we were reluctant to talk to our friends about receiving the food because of our misplaced pride. We learned later that our friends and/or schoolmates were receiving the free food as well.

Light (or loaf of) bread

Light bread was what we called sliced bread bought from a store. It was a rarity in our house. We cooked our own biscuit and corn bread. It was a treat if we managed to obtain a loaf of bread. This was such a treat that at times we ate the bread all by itself. Life didn't get much better than that. Apparently, somewhere along the way, sliced bread became sort of a standard by which other creations/inventions were compared. Thus, the expression "The greatest thing since sliced bread".

Yeast rolls

Talk about dying and going to Heaven! Several times during the course of a year, mom would bake fresh rolls from scratch. This would be a multi-day activity. The first step would be making the dough that included yeast. The dough would sit before being kneaded. The sitting/kneading cycle might be repeated before the dough was separated into small pieces that would be baked as individual rolls. The smell of fresh rolls would permeate the house. We can still smell the aroma of those rolls today. Thank you, mom!

Mom made stomach-filling, good tasting biscuits. If mom did not want to spend the time making biscuits from scratch or a sibling wanted to cook but didn't quite have the hang of making biscuits, then they made hoe cakes. It was biscuit-like bread made into one large piece in a skillet, and cooked on top of the stove. The other bread was the flap jack. Unlike biscuits or hoe cakes that were made into/from dough, the flap jack was poured into the skillet. It was a pancake of sort without the special batter. We never had pancakes made from the store-bought mix.

Biscuits, flap jacks, yeast rolls, hoe cakes were eaten as they were cooked but along with other foods. Invariably they would be used at times to make a sandwich, most often in concert with a meat: sausage, fatback, strickalean (cousins to bacon), salmon, etc. Peanut butter and jelly were also options. However, there were times when food was temporarily scarce and we (more than likely our parents) wondered where the next meal was coming from. We, kids in particular, made sandwiches with one of the breads mentioned above and only a slice of tomato, or bread and some sandwich spread, or just bread and mayonnaise or just jelly. If we had nothing to make the sandwich with other than the bread, we referred to that as an 'air sandwich'.

One of our favorite drinks was Sassafras tea. Sassafras tea was made from the root of the tree by the same name. Generally, we would find pieces of the root on top of the ground where land has been dug up/cultivated. The root has a distinctive smell about it. Typically, live trees were not very big in size. With a little experience they were easily identified. The tree root would often be laid up to dry out. The dried root was boiled and sugar was added if desired. Delicious, lip-smacking tea was made and enjoyed! The sassafras tea was a rivaled to the other favorite farm drink; red Kool-Aid.

Polk salad was a vegetable like greens that grew wild (no planting/cultivation). At times mom would mix it with the regular greens in order to make the pot a bit fuller.

The more traditional meats (poultry and pork) were augmented by wild games such as rabbits, squirrels, racoons, opossums, deer, and birds. Each was delicious, especially when cooked with sautéed onions and mom's special gravy that she put her foot in. The wild games were obtained by hunting.

A big aspect of Christmas was the food prepared in advance of Christmas day. Mom, and the women of other households, would bake cakes, pies, and prepare other food items for days. A staple and favorite of many was homemade hog-head souse/hog-head cheese. Cakes and pies were made from scratch including the icings; no canned frosting here. Our favorite cakes included the ones iced with chocolate, coconut, or pineapples. To this day we still jockey for pieces of a caramel iced cake. It was the pound cake that we would be admonished to "stop running through this house before you cause my cake to drop." Apple and peach pies or cobblers were also favored. Mom also made a large pan of chicken dressing that was to die for. It melted in your mouth with or without cranberry sauce. It is worth mentioning that the coconut was often still in the hard shell and had to be cracked open and grated in order to make the flakes. A small amount may have been diverted from the cake and eaten directly. Eat too much of the raw delight, your indiscretion would likely come to light as it often resulted in diarrhea.

There was a plant that grew wild, we called it Sheeshaw. Admittedly, we are not sure of the spelling nor the pronunciation. It looked much like the clover plant. It had a red stem above ground. We would grab a handful, chew them up, swallow the juice, and spit out the remnants. Similar to Muscadines and grapes, we would use them to ferment in water and make some 'po-man' wine.

Milk-and-Bread

A food that a child could make for themselves would be the 'milk-and-bread'. Grownups enjoyed it as well. It was kind of like having a bowl of cereal. One would crumble cornbread up into a bowl and wet it down with plain milk or buttermilk; adding sugar was optional. It was a tasty snack that could be prepared quickly, assuming that some cornbread was leftover. Some of us have admitted to trying it with modern-day cornbread mixes.

CHAPTER FIVE

Fire and Water

FIRE

We used wood to make fires, even as a number of families began to use at least a combination of wood and gas. The wood was readily available and inexpensive, but it was labor intensive. Wood-based fire was used for the stove. Wood was also used in the fireplace and heaters to heat the house during the cold months. Those same fires would typically be used to heat water for many uses, such as washing clothes. Outside fires would be used to heat water as well, and to aid in the hog-killing process, and in other ways, such as making cracklings from portions of the same hogs. Potatoes (white or sweet) cooked in the fireplace, wrapped in ashes with hot coal piled on top was a way of cooking them without starting a separate fire in the wood stove. Starting a fire had its own challenge and was not something left to the uninitiated. Starting a fire from scratch usually required some kind of kindling, a piece of paper, and an ignition source; say a match. It would be helpful to have a couple of small pieces of wood that would ignite easily (e.g. dried pine or cedar). We loved to have some discarded pieces of wood material from the "picture frame" factory. A cardinal rule of house fires, particularly in the fireplace and heaters, is never let it go completely out. It's like being a chain smoker who lights the new cigarette with the old one. Another down side to the wood burning fire was the ash that would have to be removed from the stove, heaters, and even from the outside locations. That also meant that the fire must be allowed to burn completely out at some point. While pine is good for starting fires, it also burns quickly relative to other preferred trees like Oak, Elm, Sycamore, etc. that does not burn up so quickly. A good fire in the fireplace had to have a "back stick". This would be the biggest piece practical, placed in the back of the fireplace. This would be analogous to a piece of 'block ice' in an ice chest. The cold (near freezing) water chills the drinks, but the block of ice provides the staying power.

WATER

Cistern

Prior to building our own house, we did not have running water. The one we built would have been the fourth and final home we lived in as children. One or more of the earlier houses had a cistern. A cistern provided a means of capturing rain water for subsequent use. This typically meant that the house did not have running water, nor a well, nor any other immediate means of obtaining water for washing, cooking, hygiene, etc. The homeowner, or tenant, would dig a hole in the ground in close proximity to the house. Rain water would be directed to the cistern as it rolled off the (typically tin-topped) house. Ideally the hole dug in the ground would be given a coat of cement to stabilize the dirt and keep the ground from dirtying up the water. The hole often looked like a light bulb, that is, the bottom (bulb) would have a larger diameter than the part of the hole that rose to the top of the ground. A cement cylindrical foundation would be built around the hole above ground. Attached to the cement cylinder would be a wooden cover that reduced the amount of debris that could get into the cistern. The cover did not block rain water from going into the cistern. The cover would have a door that allow for the lowering of a bucket (attached to a rope) into the cistern to retrieve water as needed. Fancier cistern setups might have a pulley system to aid in lifting of the water bucket.

The Pump

A person with sufficient resources could have a well dug and a pump system added. An individual would manually pump the attached handle until water ran out of the spicket. While this was a reliable source of water, the water still had to be carried to the house. Of course, the well would be placed as close as practical to the house. In some instances, such a well was put in place for an entire community. NOTE: a somewhat similar well (without the manual pump) is constructed for modern homes that are not privy to a community or municipality water supply.

Other Sources

Catching rain water in a 50-gallon barrel or metal drum could provide water for a few days. Other sources of water, would be to haul it from a pond, creek, or a spring. The spring was sometime associated with a creek, but not always. In one actual scenario, an opened top enclosure was erected over/around a natural spring. This allowed the water to build up to a height so that it could easily be taken from the spring and transferred to a container of choice. The water in the creek ran at a shallow height. One would have to locate a depression or make one in the creek so that a sufficient amount of water could be scooped up with a bucket. Care had to be taken in creeks as some spots in the sand were "quicksand". The quicksand we encountered was rarely as unforgiving as that in the movies, but we knew not to take any chances.

Bathrooms

Not having running water, in the early homes, precluded us from having an inside bathroom. Washing, and washing up was a chore. The first chore was obtaining hot water. Early on we heated water on top of the wood-burning stove, and sometime on the heater. Imagine trying to heat enough water for five to ten people to wash up or bath. The top of the stove was where food was being cooked as well. Water was typically heated in a black cast iron kettle (couple of gallons) and a foot tub (5 gallons). Though an elongated bath tub was manufactured, we did not have one. The primary bathing apparatus was the same round number-three tub used to wash clothes. Secondarily, we used the "foot tub" which was also used to heat water and to literally wash feet. Presumably it was the number one (#1) round galvanized tub. With a number of persons needing to clean up at the same time, someone was relegated to using the wash pan. The wash pan was typically used to wash one's hands and/or face. Cleaning up using a wash pan or the foot tub is somewhat analogous to as a sponge bath, however, no sponge was involved when we did it. With a gallon (or so) of warm water, a face towel, and a bar of soap, one would wash their face and then their underarm. Finally, the genital area and the butt was washed while squatting over the wash pan/foot tub. These clean-up efforts took place in whatever room a little privacy could be had, typically one of the bedrooms.

Of course, when working in the field we were rarely close enough to the house such that we could have run home to use the bathroom, even if we had one. One would find whatever privacy they could, wherever they could, to do a number-one or a number-two. More often then not, toilet paper was not readily available. One might be relegated to grabbing a hand full of leaves, corn shucks, etc. in order to complete their business.

Folks took water to the field in a jug. If the field was close to a creek or a natural spring, someone might fetch water in a bucket so the workers could have a cool drink. Folks did not mind drinking from the bucket using a common long-handled dipper, no matter how many individuals had preceded them. Occasionally someone would break out one of those collapsible, metal drinking cups, that when closed would collapse to a fraction of the opened height.

CHAPTER SIX

Clothing

C lothing was optional for infants and toddlers while at home. It was normal for a two-year old to be running around the house naked as a jay bird. If they were not naked, they would likely have on only a diaper or underwear. The beginning of the school year was the time to spruce up the old wardrobe, at least for school-aged children. We bought some clothing new. However, we wore hand-me-downs, passed from one sibling to another. Occasionally we received a box of donated clothes. Our angel would sometimes surprise us with a special piece of clothing. Although clothing is sometimes cyclic, not everything has the same number of lives. Women clothing generally was more varied in term of available styles. The standard outfit for males was a pair of blue jeans and the 'checkered' flannel shirt. Grown men often wore overalls (at times pronounced overhauls). The Sunday-go-to-church (or special occasion) ensemble might include a white or pastel shirt, a hook-on neck tie, and a pair of loafers. It was a pair of high-top leather shoes for work and school. When at home or in the company of close relatives, young folk generally went bare feet as much as practical; so dusty feet was the rule rather than the exception; for that matter, dusty shoes as well. Sometimes our shoes would have a big hole in the bottom. The fix would be to put some cardboard in the bottom of the shoes. The next level of repair would be when our father would put a piece of leather on the outer part of the soles of the shoes. Not sure if all families had one, but we actually had a lathe used in shoe repair. At some point during the school year, the boys might obtain a suit or separates that included a jacket. The early seventies saw the arrival of stretch knit pants, shirts with big collars, and platform shoes.

Ladies clothing was on a different plane. There was the Shift, the Tent, pleated skirt, Knee Knocker, Pedal Pushers, Cool-locks, blue jean shorts, and hot pants (even before there were daisy dukes). Many of these would be handed down to the younger sister once the original owner outgrew or got tired of them. In addition to the outer garments there was way more undergarments then males had to contend with: half and whole slips, regular or panty gridles, garters, bloomers, stockings, the works! Female clothes were plenteous because females often sewed their clothing using the sewing machine. The non-electric machine had a rocker foot pedal. Sometime the clothes were fashioned from patterns, otherwise it was simply a matter of memory and skills. Our oldest sister could make a sewing machine hum. Another lady's fashion was wearing scarfs on the head and around the neck. The scarfs and head rags were sometime used inter-changeably to enhance an outfit.

As young folks, when we got a dollar or two of our own, we began to purchase pieces of clothing here and there. Often, we could not afford to buy the item we desired. Some stores would allow us to put items on "Lay-A-Way". It was a way of buying an item on a payment plan. The items had to be completely paid off before taking possession. In recent memory, K-Mart was known to allow Lay-A-Ways.

CHAPTER SEVEN

Houses

A ll of our early houses were substandard even for the time. The one we built in the early seventies with our own hands was a giant leap forward; however, even it lacked the completeness of a professionally constructed house. All of our houses were wood framed and elevated off the ground a couple of feet or more (at least on one corner). That meant at some point having to crawl underneath to retrieve a toy or something. Like most houses of the era, in rural areas, our houses had a front porch. Some era houses had a back porch as well as a front porch; not ours. Our first two homes did not have electricity. Therefore, kerosene or coal oil lamps were used to provide light after dark. Wood burning stoves and heater were used for cooking and heating the houses. One of the most important aspects of housing is having a safe and comfortable place to sleep. With as many as twelve individuals living in a house at the same time, the sleeping arrangements left something to be desired. At times, as many as four individuals would sleep together in a full-size bed. The siblings would be arranged head-to-toe times two. It was not so bad as long as no one had smelly feet. In addition to removing the dirt of the day, this may explain why we washed our feet even if we didn't wash any other part of the body that day. When there was no longer room in a bed, we slept on the floor. A quilt or a blanket or both on the floor made for a bed substitute we referred to as a pallet. Think of it as sleeping on an ultra-firm mattress.

When the family occupied the first house in the early sixties, it initially was one large room and a kitchen. A medium size room was subsequently added. Up to twelve individuals lived in the house at one time or another. This would have included our parents, and children ranging in age from an infant through young adulthood. The second house in the early to mid-sixties had an interesting aspect in that it was divided into two halves separated by an open-air hallway. The kitchen and a bedroom were on one side of the hallway while a second bedrooms was on the opposite side. It was elevated off the ground as well. The family spent two years in this house. We recall that an uncle had a similarly constructed house. The largest number of siblings spent more years in house number three than any of the other houses. The family occupied this house from the mid-sixties until the early seventies. The house was high enough off the ground that it was fairly easy to crawl underneath it from one side to the opposite side. It had a porch that ran the length of the front of the house. It was only a few yards from a creek that was generally quiet but occasionally threatened to overflow due to a heavy rain. There were twelve individuals in the house at one time as well; however, by this time the older siblings had begun to leave the nest. A portion of the front of the house had the look of a log cabin (logs were visible). The house had only four rooms and a small storage attachment; yet this was an improvement in our situation. What was the primary room, had the main entry door, a fireplace and two full-size beds. A second room also had to two full-size beds, a wood heater, and an entry/exit door from the porch. The third smaller room did not have a window but rather a window-size opening with a hinged wooden closure. This smaller room did not have a ceiling; the tin roof was visible from the inside and was the only buffer from the elements. The fourth and final room was the kitchen/dining area. It had a wood-burning stove. On the upside, this house did have electricity. In 1972 we started construction on what would be our last family home. This would be a modern house where our family would own both the house and the land it sat on. It was also elevated off the ground. The men and boys of the family cut the trees and carried them to the sawmill and had them cut into foundation members that were very large in cross-section and of varying lengths. A neighbor who had built his own house served as the lead carpenter. Our father continued to work his 'day job' while the boys that were still living at home worked with the carpenter.

We often walked the 5 or 6 miles between where we lived and where the construction was taking place. The house was no real estate showcase but it was ours. It was great that our mother was able to get to reside in it before she transitioned to be with the Lord. The house, for all of its glory, was forever a work in progress. The first indoor bathrooms we enjoyed was forever evolving; however, we no longer had to go outside to the outhouse. There was the addition of a garage although we never parked an operational vehicle in it. The garage had the dual barn doors. We are not sure, but this house maybe the only one that we lived in that is still standing.

Shotgun House

Our primary family home was never constructed in this style. This style was more appropriate for a small family. We had neighbors and relatives that lived in this style of house. There would typically be three room of similar dimensions lined up in a row from front to back. The last of the three rooms was typically designated as the kitchen.

The Out House

We recall the nostalgic question, "do you recall when toilet paper had beautiful prints?" We chuckled as it occurred to us that our toilet paper had print but it was news print. The toilet paper substitute was actual newspaper. That was some of our best toilet paper because it could be made softer/palatable by balling it up and un-balling it.

Some of the worse tissue substitutes were the catalogs we received from the nationally renowned stores. Their catalogs were typically made of glossy pages which were not highly conducive to personal hygiene. Even more interesting is where all of this occurred as we did not have an inside bathroom until the early seventies. At different times we used an outhouse, a pot, slop-jar, and the great outdoors. Many people are familiar with the outhouse by virtue of its portrayal on television and in the movies. Conceptually it is the early version of the porta potty, yet different. The primary difference is that outhouses are not portable. Somewhere along the way there was an out-house that had two (twin) seats. There is no recollection of two people ever using it at the same time. At times we would be afraid to use the outhouse for fear that a rodent, a snake, or some other critter might be hiding inside. The pot was approximately nine inches tall, nine inches in diameter (ten-inch flare at the top) with a lid that simply lay atop of it. The lid could not completely hold down the smell. The pot had a handle like a bucket. It was generally used at night or by someone ill and unable to go to the outhouse or out into the woods. The pot was constructed of white enamel similar to that of the wash pan used for washing hands and face and taking sponge baths.

Smoke House

In this context, the smoke house is not really a house at all. It was a house-like structure where meats would be hung and smoked for preservation/taste.

Hen House

It is lumped here only by virtue of the name. This is where chickens would spend the night, or where they sheltered during bad weather. It was in no way climate controlled. There was a ledge four to five feet up where the chicken actually sat (and presumably) slept during the night; also, where they laid eggs. The floor (ground) was covered with feces. You might want to pinch your nose if you needed to enter. The dried fecal matter would be harvested on occasion to be used as a natural fertilizer.

Barn

A barn is a building (house of sort) where livestock was able to come in out of the weather; where hay and other forms of food for animals; and, where farm equipment was stored. It was probably a good place to obtain some natural fertilizer as well. As life would have it, some folks' barn rivaled one or more of the houses that we lived in.

It was unlikely that the construction of an outhouse, a smoke house, a hen house, nor a barn had to meet any building codes.

CHAPTER EIGHT

School

S chool varied quite a bit across the span of siblings. The eldest attended the one or two-room school house with a pot-belly stove. The youngest children got the benefit of head start and kindergarten. We always wanted to go to school. Our county's schools were essentially segregated until the fall of 1969, although there had been minor attempts at integration earlier. The teachers were nice for the most part. Even the ones we thought were mean or stern or firm, had our best interest at heart. Corporal punishment was part of business as usual when students fail to obey the rules. The bus rides of the sixties and seventies were not much different from bus rides of today. It was rare but occasionally a fight would breakout. One scenario was that as we and our bus cohorts completed the eighth grade at the elementary school, we would catch a bus from the same elementary school to the high school which was located, a dozen or so miles away. While in elementary school, we brought our lunch to school as there was no cafeteria. Lunch, like many other aspects of life, was indicative of the family's socio-economic status. Some students had cold-cut sandwiches while others had low-grade salmon patties or fatback biscuits. We are sure we called the patties 'Simon'. At some point one of the schools used student-labor to make bologna sandwiches that were provided free to students. We were excited to receive a sandwich and a box of milk. Also, we recited the Pledge of Allegiance and sang the Battle Hymn of the Republic each morning before the start of classes. Interestingly enough, we were given the New Testament, a little red book about 5x3x0.5 inches in size. We had a number of activities at school. A favorite activity or time of year would be the celebration of "May Day", that included the more memorable game of platting the May Pole. We exchanged simple Christmas gifts. We participated in the annual fundraiser for the March of Dimes. Students were given a money-holder card with slots to hold the donated dimes. Another memorable event was, once when the girls' bathroom was not working, they took over the boys' bathroom. The boys went to the bathroom in the woods that day. Guess it would have been too hard to schedule alternating times for each to use the one bathroom. Also, during those rare days when there was no field work to be done at home, we might be allowed to go home with a schoolmate and spend the night; a sleep-over. In some cases that meant taking a different school bus; which could be interesting for multiple reasons. Not the least of which, your nemesis might ride that bus. No one remembers the logistics of those overnight visits. Did we carry a change of clothes? If so, what did we put them in? In any case, our friends would reciprocate and spend the night at our house at some point. We would juggle bed assignments for that one night. At the onset of integration, what had been our primary elementary/middle school was closed. The high school had white administrators and a significant number of white teachers. For the most part, both teachers and students were respectful of each other. High school sport was primarily limited to football and basketball. Band was also available as an extracurricular activity. The band performed at football games during half-time and we participated in the annual Christmas parade in a sister city. A couple of standard high school activities were the leaf collections and the insect collections. The insects were attached to a piece of cardboard with stick pins. The leaf collection involved securing the leaves using wax paper. In both cases we had to provide the common name and the scientific name. We can name many trees today because of that exercise; insects not so much. Occasionally, we would be given actual paper covers to protect the school books. If we did not have 'official' book covers, we would make our own from whatever materials we could get our hands on. Brown paper bags from the grocery store were sturdy and made the best book covers. One could write pretty much anything they wanted on the covers. There was unwritten rules of decency. A favorite would be a heart drawn with the name of the student and the name of their (real or imaginary) boyfriend or girlfriend.

Generally, we did good in school. Missing a significant number of school days working on the farm some time caused some of us to not be promoted each year. However, we were committed to getting an education. Fourteen of fifteen siblings received their high school diploma or equivalent. Five siblings went to college directly out of high school and earned at least the bachelor degree; some a masters. We were excited to go off to college and pursue career choices that would be far removed from our farm-work days. Some earned their degree by going to college part time over a number of years. Thanks God for college financial aid; the Basic Education Opportunity Grant and the Supplemental Education Opportunity Grant and work-study. A college education is not the answer for everyone, but for many individuals and families it was essential. To help young people, from the neighborhood and elsewhere, pursue a college education, our family established and continue to fund an endowed scholarship in our parents' name. The scholarship is connected to Mississippi Valley State University (MVSU), the college that multiple siblings attended and received their undergraduate degrees.

Since we did not have streets, we probably could not have been considered 'street-wise'. We probably were not 'dirty-road-wise' either. How did we get 'life' education, which was not available in the classroom? Our parents encouraged formal education. Education beyond that was in short supply. For example, "The Talk", as it were, never took place. Subjects like puberty, sex, pregnancy, etc. were never discussed. On at least one occasion, while watching a couple kiss passionately on TV, our father exclaimed (upon entering the room), "what are they doing, biting?" Of course, we didn't answer. If a TV program was considered too racy, we would be told to turn the TV off and read a book; sometime that might be an encyclopedia.

CHAPTER NINE

Church

Our family attended an African Methodist Episcopal (AME) church. It was basically a one-room, wood-framed, white building. The building did not have air conditioning. It had a somewhat vaulted ceiling but no ceiling fans. The building had a wood-burning, potbelly heater. This meant that in the winter we braved the cold until a fire was started and the heat began to circulate. At that time the church did not have an inside bathroom but rather an outhouse. The church had a graveyard or cemetery nearby. The membership was comprised of a half-dozen or so families plus a hand full of individuals from the surrounding community. The pastor came one Sunday out of the month. Typically, that was the third (pastoral) Sunday. The pastor generally served for three to four years. Sunday school classes were held on all Sundays. A collection or offering was always taken. Children contributed whatever coins that had been given to them. Adults may have contributed currency; a dollar or so. As each individual put their contribution in the basket, they would utter a biblically related phrase such as, "Jesus wept", "It is more blessed to give than to receive", "The Lord is my Shepherd", etc. or maybe one of the ten commandments. We always sang a portion of a hymn that we had been taught. We do not recall having hymn books. Adults appeared to enjoy meter music while the youth prayed that it would be over sooner than later. This was singing whereby the leader would recite the words for a portion of a song. Then the rest of the congregation would sing those words in a long, drawn out tempo. This would continue in a sequential manner until one or more verses were completed. A couple of times each year there would be a celebration that would be accompanied by food prepared by the membership and guests. Typical celebrations might correspond to Easter, Mothers' or Fathers' Day, and "Children's Day". Other churches were invited to participate on these special occasions; especially churches on the same circuit. Of course, those churches expected us to reciprocate when they had special events. Often time if a community church could not have members of their congregation participate substantially, they would send a monetary gift offering. Our church would do likewise. On Children's Day, the children sang, recited poems, read scripture, etc. Church was the place that we would wear our best clothing – 'Sunday best'. For many years the ride to Church (as well as other places) was in the bed of our pickup truck, once the cab was full. These trips were along dirt roads. The vehicle created a dust storm of sort as it traveled along the road. The dust would disperse in all directions. When the vehicle came to a stop, much of the dust would catch up to and cover the vehicle. The individuals that rode in the back of our truck, particularly girls, would wear a light cover over their clothing to keep from being dusty when we arrive at church – thus the term "duster". Many of those dirt-only roads still exist even today. At times our truck or even the car allowed dust into the interior portion of the vehicle. Therefore, some level of tidying up was required upon arriving to church. Typically, once a year in the summer or fall, churches would have Revival. This would be a week of evening services (not including Saturday and Sunday), perhaps with a guest preacher. At some point during that week of services, parents would send their teenaged or pre-teen children to sit on the front-most pew, or the mourner's bench. This was a prelude to the child joining the church and being baptized at the end of the revival. Our guess is that most of the children had not developed a real appreciation for what they were entering into. The same lack of appreciation persist for many youngsters even today. We were taught to say a prayer before meals, before going to bed, and taught the Lord's prayer. Our dad would tell us to go and read the Bible if he thought we were watching too much television.

Church essentially got started as we prepared and got dressed at home on Sunday mornings. We turned on the radio, static and all, and listened to gospel music. Radio had grown since our early days of tuning in. Much of the Sunday morning music was provided by local folks that had formed groups. These soloists, duets, trios, quartets would be live in the local radio station. They even did Public Service Announcements, particularly where they and others would be performing, which churches had a program scheduled, etc. We fondly recall one furniture store that would say "wear your coat, there is no heat". Guess that was just their winter advertisement.

On the Sundays the preacher came to our church, he would occasionally dine at a member's house. This was common for circuit pastors of rural churches. Fairly or unfairly, it became a standing rumor that the preachers always ate the choice pieces of food, particularly the chicken. Therefore, the host family, the children in particular, would get to eat whatever remained. The stories took a life of their own; someone had only the chicken back, or even the chicken feet to eat. The story really has gone too far if the story teller claims that someone ate the part of the chicken that held the tail feathers. We called it the bomb-ma-nob.

CHAPTER TEN

Transportation

This chapter was originally titled "Automobiles". However, we used several, including near primitive, modes of getting from one place to another. Thus, the title "Transportation".

In general, our automobiles were at least 10 years old when we purchased them. Not many, if any, individuals or families purchased automobiles of the showroom floor. Each family (father) had their favorite automobile nameplate. Four-door sedans were more practical for transporting people. Of course, we had a couple of pickup trucks as they were more of a necessity for farm work. The navy blue 1953 pickup was one of the earlier ones. Trucks were often preferred over cars because one could haul more stuff. The equipment was probably pretty standard. Ironically, the transmission type was referred to as "standard shift". What is now referred to as a stick shift or simply a manual transmission. The rods that formed part of the truck's clutch and brake pedals disappeared into the floor when pressed. The starter was a spring-loaded, foot-operated gizmo adjacent to the accelerator. At that time pick-up trucks typically had one rear tail light that was mounted in concert with the license plate (tag) attachment. The tail light/tag ensemble was on the extreme left or right rear. At times we would have way more individuals piled into the cab of the truck then would be allowed today. At other times we would pile into the bed of the truck, happy to go to the neighborhood store or into town. We enjoyed the breeze of riding in the truck bed. Presumably for convenience sake, lots of folks turned the area inside the cab and beneath the windshield into a make-shift filing cabinet. To ask a person for a receipt, a bill that was due, or an important letter, meant a trip out to the vehicle to rummage through those papers in the windshield. When a vehicle with a manual transmission would not start, and the problem appeared to be starter or battery related, we would tow or push the vehicle to jump-start it by popping the clutch. If there were a minimum number of individuals for the pushing technique, the driver would push while running alongside the vehicle with the door open and jump in once a sufficient speed was achieved. If the issue was not repaired over the course of days/weeks, we would practice parking the vehicle on a hill in order for gravity to assist with the 'push-to-start' process. This technique was problematic and thus not recommended for vehicles with automatic transmissions. It was also common to tow one vehicle with a similar vehicle (no tow truck). The two vehicles would be connected by mean of a chain or rope. A second person would steer and brake the towed vehicle that was towed with its gear in neutral. The prognosis was generally not good if one had to resort to towing to facilitate a jump-start. Most automobiles had a hood ornament. At one time or another we had a 61 through 65 sedan or station wagon of the same nameplate. Working at an automobile dealership, our father would occasionally bring home an interesting vehicle. We recall one vehicle that had push-buttons gear shifters. It was a very large car with pronounced tail fins.

Like a number of neighbors, we had a couple of old cars on the property where we lived that we played in as children. Maybe one that we added to the collection; another that preceded our move onto the property. They were the kind of vehicles that in the right hands, would have become a collector's item. At some point the automobile became more than just the family car or the pickup truck used to haul pretty much anything. Young men, and in some cases not so young men, began to 'soup up' their cars. A cousin to the 'trick out my ride' that came along years later. The early souped up cars typically had a V-8 engine. Guys would install dual exhaust out the back end, add things like dressed up wheels (mags), an after-market 4-barrel carburetor, curb feelers, a curb knob, and dual antennas, even if there was no radio. A hand full of models were adorned with fender skirts that covered a portion of the rear wheel wells.

To further differentiate from the family car, young men preferred, 2-door hardtops over the 4-door sedan. A 4-door hardtop might be acceptable in a pinch. The term hard top might sound misleading. It meant that there was no partition between the front and rear, side windows. This was not the case for the sedan. So, to make it even more confusing, by definition, the convertible was a 'hardtop'. Convertibles were not all that popular. That was probably because of all the dust to be dealt with on the rural roads.

The curb knob allowed the driver to steering and easily make turns using only one hand. It too was pretty much window dressing. Reportedly, it has been outlawed except as an aid for drivers with a physical disability. The curb knob could essentially only be used in conjunct with power steering. The curb feelers were probably 50% functional and 50% decorative. At least in theory, you could hear them contact the curb and avoid scuffing up the car's tires and rims.

In large part thanks to the movie Shaft and its theme song, folk with disposable income might go for the diamond in the back, and the sunroof top. If you really wanted to be the talk of the town, there was the capability to have a TV in your ride. On the other hand, you could just fake it and install what looked like a TV antenna. That would sufficiently impress some folks.

The evolution of the automotive entertainment system somewhat mirrored home entertainment. There was the AM/FM radio, then came the 8-track tape player followed by the cassette player. The CD player and MP3 devices represent a totally different age. Other features that made a different to car enthusiasts included bucket seats, stick shift or manual transmission (three or four in floor), power steering, and oh yeah – air conditioning. There seem to be no limit to the number of possible options. The decorative touch for many was a set of fuzzy dice hanging from the review mirror.

Any vehicles in the category 'car-truck' that are still around, likely qualify as a classic as they have not been made for a number of years. This class of vehicles had a sedan-like front half but had a cargo bed for the rear half; much like the rear half of a pickup truck, but with a lower profile.

Although our tractors, horses, and mules were primarily used for work, they were also used for a ride to a nearby destination. Anything to avoid walking! The mule or horse would be ridden with a saddle, a blanket, or completely bare back. Riding bare back, particularly for a prolonged period of time, often proved to be painful for the backside of the rider and often left the rider smelling like the animal ridden.

The horse and/or mule, donning a full set of gear, would often be used to pull a slide. A slide would typically be a 4-feet wide by 6-feet long wooden platform. The platform would be attached to the edge of two 2 by 6-inch boards; the opposing edges would 'slide' along the ground; somewhat analogous to a sled pulled by dogs in the Iditarod. The forward end of the 2 by 6 would be cut at an angle (e.g. 45 degrees). The slide would be used to transport one or two persons and some cargo. It might be used to transverse terrain that was not ideal for an automobile; hauling a barrel of water from the creek or pond, or pulling a load of firewood out of the forest.

A tandem of horses, mules, or a combination, geared down would also be used to pull a 4-wheeled wagon. The wagon would be used to transport people, crops, wood, etc.

The simplest form of transportation was referred to as "Uncle Walker's pickup". That was a joking way of saying, to get from point A to point B by walking; picking up your feet.

CHAPTER ELEVEN

Holidays

We did not routinely observe or celebrate most of the calendar holidays. On the farm, New Year's Day was just another day. Presidents day, Memorial Day, Independence Day, Labor Day, Veterans Day, and Thanksgiving were work-days, especially if they fell on Monday through Saturday. We were excited when Christmas rolled around, for it was the one holiday we celebrated. It got favor from adults because it was a Christian holiday. For that same reason, Easter was a time for celebration although it was not an official holiday in the truest sense, and it always fell on a Sunday. Thanksgiving may have gotten a tad more attention. A few families actually raised turkeys.

New Year's Day

There was no emotional attachment to New Year's Day. It registers because somewhere along the way certain foods became associated with it. Rightly so, this should be couched along with the other superstitions, but here we go. If food was prepared corresponding to the colors of money, you would in turn be blessed with money during the course of the year. Greens (Collards, Turnips, Mustards, etc.) represented paper money (dollar bills). Chitterlings and hog maw represented silver coins, and brown beans/peas represented copper coins (pennies). This cultural practice continues to be practiced by many households, albeit without the expectation of the money blessing. We have heard different explanation of the meaning behind the various food choices for New Year's Day. We do not claim to be an authority on the subject. It should be noted that Chitterlings for some are Chitlins for others. There are those who prefer mustard with theirs while other swear by hot sauce.

Easter

Easter got some attention, not so much as a holiday but as a Christian observance. Church service was the order of the day on Easter Sunday. Typically, there was a special program for Easter. That program usually involved children giving speeches and recitations. Although the bunny was not all that prominent, Easter eggs were. We did not have to paint eggs but we had fun hiding them, hunting for them, and eating them. Leading up to Easter, there was some homage paid to Good Friday. Maybe we ate some fish from the pond. The elders seemed more bent on getting certain vegetables planted on or around good Friday. The seasonally related Palm Sunday was not observed to the degree it is today.

Christmas

Christmas was the only holiday that really excited us as children. Though Christmas is a Christian holiday for many, there was not a lot of churchy hoopla, not beyond the angel on top of the Christmas tree. We lived in the rural, so we did not buy Christmas trees. We took a few steps into the woods and cut down our Christmas tree. The preferred tree was cedar, and they were plentiful. Pine was probably a distance second. The tree was decorated much like it is today. It seems like 'angel hair' and lights were used more extensively. There were no gifts under the tree. We put our shoeboxes under the tree on Christmas eve so that Santa would put gifts in the boxes for us. The boxes were somewhat analogous to Christmas stockings except that stockings tend to be for small secondary type gifts. The boxes held the primary Christmas gifts unless they would not fit into the boxes. We were conditioned not to expect anything too substantial. Everyone would receive in their box, a standard set of Christmas treats such as an apple, an orange, a number of pecans, English walnuts, Brazil nuts, peppermint sticks, and some of the chocolate bells in foil wrapping, and sometimes a small toy. There would generally be extra nuts available in the house along with some of the orange sliced candy. It was probably made from lots of sugar and was even covered with grains of sugar. Girls often received dolls of some kind while boys often received poorly constructed cap pistols. Once you were old enough, you might receive firecrackers and other assorted firework (sparklers, roman candles, etc.). We were not allowed to set off firework (especially the noisy ones) until the day after Christmas. Not sure if we ever receive anything substantial for Christmas like a bicycle. At some point the Box Project program became a benefactor for the family. We did not know much about it, but it provided gifts and clothing throughout the year for birthdays, and especially at Christmas. More about our angel and the Box Project later.

Gifts were not readily exchanged between family and friends. There was some minimal exchange of gifts at school. The least favorite gift was the chocolate covered cherries, which had some milky white candy between the cherry and the chocolate shell. Lots of people gave them. Perhaps they were both plentiful and inexpensive.

A big deal at Christmas was the food prepared in advance of Christmas day. Mom, and the women of other households, would bake cakes, pies, and prepare other food items like it was nobody's business.

The annual Christmas parade was a big deal for children of all ages. We would wrap up in layers of clothing, stand on city streets (often in the cold) and watch high school bands and the local college (MVSU) band march and perform along the parade route. The floats were not too shabby either.

CHAPTER TWELVE

Fun/ Entertainment

As kids, our biggest source of entertainment was probably our own antics. Children enjoyed sitting around playing games and talking when not working in the field. During the early years we did not have electricity, so no radio, no television, etc. We did get electricity in the mid-sixties. With that came radio. We were able to listen to music over the airways. We could access only a couple of interesting Radio stations. By default, we were exposed to a variety of music whether we wanted to be or not. We could sing along with the likes of Johnny Cash, Elvis Pressley, Charlie Pride, and we were familiar with songs like "A Boy Name Sue", "Kiss an Angel Good Morning", and an "Ode to Billie Joe" just to mention a few. There was a station in Nashville that played some music more to our liking. There is a vague recollection of a disc jockey that had the word 'horse' in his on-air name. Late at night we were introduced to another on-air personality that would howl like a wolf. Later we got wind of WDIA in Memphis. A favorite on this station was the early morning gospel segment. The radio had extra bands that allowed us to hear some TV programs even though we did not see the pictures. Some grownups listened to the soap operas. Eventually we did get a black and white television. We were thrilled to get TV and the era shows like Green Acres, Lawrence Welk, Marcus Welby, the Mod Squad, Gilligan's Island, and the FBI just to mention a few. Of course, cartoons had their place in our hearts; I'm Popeye the sailor man, toot-toot! The local TV station signed off the air by playing the National Anthem after the ten o'clock evening news. The TV had the 'rabbit ear' antenna. When an antenna ear broke we replaced it with a clothes hanger. Invariably the TV would lose a knob, typically the channel selector. That generally meant keeping a pair of pliers handy. The vise grip pliers were the preferred type.

Fishing

Fishing was an inexpensive past-time. Folks fished for the fun of it, to eat, or both. It seemed like there was always a pond or a creek (fresh water) within walking distance.

Very few individuals had fancy fishing gear such as a rod and reel. A bamboo pole (also referred to as a fishing cane) was the primary piece of gear. Some fishing line, a reasonable size hook, a floater, and a sink rounded out the components needed. Throw in some earthworms and you would be set for an afternoon of fishing. We made our share of trips to the bank of the pond. Cat fish, Trout, and Bass were the fish of choice; no Whiting, Pollock, and certainly no Tilapia. Catching them and eating them was fun, but not the cleaning of the fish. The skinning, de-scaling and the removing of the inner parts, yuck!

Bike riding

Getting a bicycle was a big deal for us. The boys more so than the girls, had fun riding them. In addition to riding them around the house, the bicycle was a means of transportation to visit friends and ride together. In addition to riding, we learn to maintain the bikes in every respect. It was a basic task to repair a flat tire. There was not any part of the single speed bike that we would not tear down and replace or rebuild. Some kids graduated to a three-speed bike that would require hand brakes on the handle bars. Not sure if anyone of our contemporaries ever owned a ten-speed bike as a kid.

Playing with toys

At times toys were bought, but many were made out of materials lying around the house. An empty match box turned nicely into a pickup truck when half opened. Ok, so it did not have wheels. You have not lived until you have fashioned a blob of mud into a toy car, toy peoples, or some other toy. You had to use your imagination! If we had a few coins, we would pick up something from the 'Five and dime' store. As we got older we bought things from mail-order catalogs. Marbles were an affordable toy mostly played with by boys. Although some kids just liked the idea of having pretty marbles even if they never played. The girls enjoyed playing with and making dolls out of sticks, horse hair, and cutting doll pictures out of catalogs. The game of Jacks was also a favorite of girls. The slingshot could be considered a toy or a weapon. In our case, the former. It was always the homemade variety for us. Grab a sufficiently sized tree limb with a branch and cut it into a "Y". Attach a piece of rubber (maybe from a tire's inner tube) to the two angled pieces, and you are ready for target practice.

Sports

We enjoyed playing basketball, football, and stick-ball. The large number of siblings came in handy at game time. The equipment rarely resembled any offi-cially sanctioned equipment. As a matter fact, at times we played three sports (base or stick ball, basketball, football) with the same piece of equipment. The most frequently available equipment substitute was the 12 oz soda can. It could be used for either sport; never mind the occasional bump on the head. Stickball was our lame attempt at baseball or softball. A nice limb from a tree, perhaps with a little fashioning made for a bat. Then it was off to the bases; no gloves in this game. Outs were based on hitting the runner with the makeshift ball. The same can would also be used as a football; go long! It was mostly tag rather than tackle. The same can would be used as the ball in our basketball game; tossing the can in an old bucket nailed up on the side of the house, or through a bicycle wheel (with all of the spokes removed) nailed onto a tree. Nets! We didn't need no stinking nets. Over time, our soda can was replaced with a round plastic or rubber ball. Maybe if someone went to a county fair, they might win or buy a souvenir baseball, basketball or football. We never had the actual dimension of a play area for either sport, but that never stopped us. Fun has never cost so little since.

Hunting

Admittedly, this was a pastime for parents (fathers) and older siblings. They would go into the woods, often at night, and hunt for rabbits, squirrels, coons, opossums, deer, birds and the like. The hunter would most likely be armed with a rifle. Our father had a single-shot 22 caliber rifle for many years. He also had a double barrel, twelve gage shot gun. The shot gun could be loaded with buckshots (shell full of small pellets) or slug shots (more of a solid load). The hunting of certain critters was confined to specific times of the year. Often a hunting license would be required. However, it was not uncommon for some folks to hunt out of season and without a license. Not necessarily a requirement, but most hunters went out with a reasonably trained dog or multiple dogs. Of course, different breeds of dog were better for specific game. The hound dogs, and the spotted bird dogs were most common. We are uncertain where cleaning and preparing the catch fell on the curve of enjoyment. In many cases the killed animal would be partially cleaned in the wood where it was killed. The more serious hunters wore camouflage clothing, although at times it was common to wear a loud colored red vest for safety reasons.

Dating

The dating scene typically involved the young man visiting the young lady at her house. The parents of the young lady pretty much needed to know the parents of the gentlemen caller. He had to arrive before dark and leave before it got too late. This in part, may have been due to the fact that the room where the couple visited together was also one of the family's bedrooms, as all rooms in the earlier homes were bedrooms except for the kitchen. The bedroom/living-room combo was also problematic when any guests, including relatives, visited. There was a period when a teenage sister would receive a male guest, our father would sit in the room with them. Invariably the young man would become uncomfortable, leave, often never to return. Rather than having a date, we would say that Susie has 'company'. The word company was also used more broadly to indicate when there were guests of any kind. Some courting took place at school, on the bus, at church, and whenever an opportunity presented itself. It was mostly good clean fun. Occasionally mother nature slipped passed the parents and other adults.

Checkers

A checker board would be drawn on a piece of cardboard. The item most often used for the checker pieces would be soda pop bottle tops. They would be turned up or down to represent the red or black checker pieces. Two of them could be easily stacked to indicate achieving a king. Almost everyone played the game at one time or another. We loved the game. Many of us still play to this very day.

Rolling store

The Rolling Store was a favorite sight to see. This was analogous to the current day ice cream truck, except it had more non-ice cream options than ice cream. No groceries, just snacks and unhealthy, great tasting items for the young and the young at heart. Cookies, nabs, peanut butter crackers, Holloway candy, kisses (4 in the pack), bubble gum, Stage Plank, Chico-Stick, and of course Pojo ice cream (or ice milk). The yellow box of Pojo ice cream came with a flat wooden 'spoon' in a sealed white paper wrapper. We probably could buy a soft drink (or soda pop) as well.

The Motorcycle

We are not sure exactly when, but at some point, we came into possession of an old, non-functioning motorcycle. Some of the weightier pieces (e.g., motor) had been removed. So, it was really the skeleton of a motorcycle. Nevertheless, we were able to ride it around the house using human power. One person would ride it while another person provided the propulsion needed to push it. The rider and pusher would change position after circling the house a few times. Sometimes the rider and/or the pusher would make sound with their mouth to imitate the sound of a functioning motorcycle. Since we were going in circle, at times the rider would lean into the curve. Those were some good times!

CHAPTER THIRTEEN

Discipline

B ehaving and minding your manners were a must in our home. Discipline started early, probably as a toddler; just a light spanking on the legs with just the fingers and an increase in the voice level. A few years later one would graduate to the good old fashion open hand spanking on the butt, then the switch (tree limb) or the belt. Mom would actually make us go and find our own switch for her to whip us. Seems like the Elm was a favorite tree for switches. Mom gave more frequent whippings but Pop gave the more severe whippings. Of course, after the whippings we would be crying, sniffling, snot-ting, etc. The person having doled out the discipline would invariably say "stop that crying or I will give you something to really cry for". In today's climate, some of the whippings would possibly be considered child abuse. However, we have yet to come across a contemporary that thinks that they were abused as a child, at least not as far as the corporal punishment. It was widely held that if you got a whipping at school, you were likely to get another one when you got home. The parent's refrain might be, "You were not sent to school to act a fool". There was the proverbial references to the woodshed. Our parents never felt the need to take us aside before administering discipline. Wherever they were when the need arose was sufficient. Additionally, we suppose the woodshed implied ready equipment for the gentle persuasion. We did not actually have a woodshed; only a wood pile. With all of this love there was no room for hate. Even older siblings would threaten to discipline the younger ones with expressions like "a hard head makes a soft behind". Think of it like tenderizing meat for cooking using the mallet-like instrument. At some point, all that was needed was 'the look' from our parents or other adults. Our father's presence was usually enough to deter us from misbehaving. In general, mothers were more than likely to be the one to inflict some discipline in the midst of bad or inappropriate behavior in order to have it cease immediately. They had this way of pinching some part of the body, often an ear. If she really wanted your attention, she would add a twist to the pinch. One would be reluctant to pull away as that made the pain worse. The pinch was a favorite of older siblings when they felt they were obliged to discipline a younger sibling. Generally speaking, discipline was swift and painful, yet children knew they were loved and cared for, even if love was not often verbalized. Physical signs of affection, such as hugs and kisses, were in short supply. It has been said that now-a-days the pendulum has swung too far in the other direction; that is, there is lots of hugs and kisses and too little discipline. Only time will tell.

Discipline at School

A paddling or whipping was part of business as usual when one fail to obey the school rules. If the teacher whipped you at school, you likely got another whipping when you got home. Whipping was serious business, nothing like the hand spanking of today. The teacher or principal used rulers, belts, straps, etc. One teacher was known for using a piece from an automobile's fan belt. She named it "Black Annie". The ex-military principal was known for making the boys do push-ups as a form of discipline. If two or more individuals were involved in some kind of infraction, they would sometime be given the option to paddle each other. The students would be admonished to get each other good or the grownup would take over and apply the paddling.

CHAPTER FOURTEEN

Medical Remedies

We did not go to the doctor at the drop of a hat. During many illnesses, we were treated naturally and with over-the-counter medicines, and went to the doctor as the last resort. Some vaccines were administered at school. As we worked in the field, we would sometimes have stomach aches (real or imaginary). Our father would have us chew on a black berry briar root to supposedly relieve the ache. Over time we came to believe that the bitter tasting root was a test to see if we really had a stomach ache, or if we were looking for an opportunity to rest in the shade or possibly get to go to the house. If you had a bad cold you could be sure that you would receive a dose of castor oil. There was also the annual dose of castor oil to clean out one's system.

We also took a medicine called 666 (or "Three sixes") as another treatment for the common cold. Part of our treatment for a cold was to have our upper body slathered with a store-bought menthol vapor rub. Anyone in the same room would get a 'contact' benefit. Something called Taler, that was made from beef fat, was a home-grown substitute. For a real upset stomach, we would often take some "pink medicine". It probably had a more official name, but pink medicine was sufficient for us. If someone was believed to be even slightly constipated, a dose of "Syrup of Black Draught" was in order. One thing about most of the remedies; their taste was often worse than the illness, especially the castor oil and cod liver oil. There was also remedies for external wounds as well. There was a concoction of kerosene and soot taken from inside the chimney. Dr. Tichenor was a staple product to have around. It served as mouthwash, as well as an antiseptic for sores or insect bites. Since it had a small alcohol content, some individuals no doubt took a swig just for the hell of it. A couple of over-the-counter remedies are no longer readily available. BC and Standback were a couple of powdered brands of aspirins. The Standback had a radio jingle – "Snap back with Standback". Several brands of aspirin could be purchased in quantities of a dozen in a flat tin. This was much more portable than the large-quantity bottles.

We are not sure if the following is a remedy or a superstition. To cure the hiccups, drink several swallows of water. If that doesn't work, have someone scare the person with the hiccups by doing something like jumping from behind a door and going "boo". How about counting to ten while holding your breath. If a person had a 'boil', he/she would be instructed to place a piece of 'fatback' meat on the location. Marcus Welby would have been proud of us. We did occasionally go to the dentist, although in some cases we took matters into our own hands. One of our dental practices was to tie one end of a piece of thread to a loose tooth, then tie the other end to a door knob; the 'patient' would stand back while we slammed the door shut. The swing of the slamming door would break the tooth free. We are still waiting for the tooth fairy to visit.

CHAPTER FIFTEEN

Superstitions

T he dictionary defines a superstition as…any belief that is inconsistent with known facts or rational thought; also, any action or practice based on such a belief.[1]

These are some of the more prominent superstitions we heard, voiced, and at times believed. Many of them were promulgated by adults, probably including our parents. Most or many of these have fallen by the way; however, a few are quoted to this day. Occasionally a person will say, I do not believe the superstition but why press my luck. Some superstitions beg for an explanation or clarification. Others can simply be taken or dismissed at face value.

A horse shoe was generally associated with good luck. Later the orientation of the shoe was said to matter; open side up or down.

You could win the race to good luck if you knocked on wood first, after you and a person with whom you were talking, uttered the same word or phrase simultaneously.

You will have good luck if you find a 4-leaf clover.

After taking a wiz, spit in your urine for good luck.

It is bad luck to walk under a ladder. This was generally an extension ladder (of sort) for us. Presumably it applies to a step ladder as well.

It is bad luck for a lady to sit her purse or hand bag on the floor.

You will have bad luck if a black cat crosses the road in front of you. Negate the bad luck by turning around and taking an alternate route.

It is bad luck if two people walking together split a pole, that is, pass the pole on opposite sides. The bad luck can be canceled if one person immediately back-tracks and then pass the pole on the same side as their companion.

It is bad luck if the Christmas tree is still up when New Year's Day arrives.

Seven years of bad luck for cracking/breaking a mirror.

Step on a crack break your mother's back. The crack is presumed to be a break as opposed to a construction joint. For example, a break in a section of side walk.

If the palm of your hand itches, you are coming into some money.

If your ear itches, someone is talking about you.

Weather-wise, the first three days of the new year will be representative of the first three months of the new year.

If the ground hog sees its shadow on ground hog day, there will be bad weather for an additional six weeks.

Lighting never strikes in the same place twice. Aside from the literal interpretation, this superstition has been generalized to mean that nothing good or bad (but particularly bad) will happen a second time like it did the first time.

Do not apply ointment or salve with the index/pointing finger.

If a finger is caught in a turtle's mouth, the turtle will hold on until it hears thunder.

If you eat a green/unripe persimmon your lips will turn inside out.

If a snake's tail is cut off, the tail will not die until after sundown.

If a Jointed snake is cut into two pieces, the two pieces can join back together later.

If the sun shines through while it is raining, the devil is beating his wife.

If a devil horse spits in your eye you will go blind. Eventually we came to know that the appropriate name for the insect is the Praying Mantis.

None of the above superstitions have been proven to be true or false. Which is in part what makes them superstition. Which also suggests that anyone can create a superstition. Try this out for size. Circle your house (dwelling), while walking backward, then howl at the moon, you will have new hair growth.

---

[1] Webster's New World Dictionary Revised Fawcett Popular Library Pocket-size Edition, Copyright 1979.

CHAPTER SIXTEEN

Sayings/ Expressions

T hese are phrases people in our "Neck of the woods" would say. They were not generally taught in school. Some are rarely used today (if ever), while other have risen to the point of routine usage. They are in no particular order. As with superstitions, some beg for clarification.

"The only things that are certain in life are death and taxes"

When someone tells you 'you have to do something', you might reply "The only things I have to do is, die and live until I die".

"The Mississippi Rule" is that "If you move you lose". This was generally applied to someone getting up, and someone else taking their seat.

A fun way to spell Mississippi. "M I crooked letter crooked letter, I crooked letter crooked letter, I hump-back humpback I."

"Beauty is only skin deep but ugly is to the bone."

"Looked" or "Looking like something the cat dragged in". Usually said of someone not looking like the best version of themselves; perhaps a bit disheveled.

"The greatest thing since sliced bread".

"Chewing the fat" refers to having a conversation (talking). "Bumping gums" is a similar expression.

"Your eyes are bigger than your stomach" is something a parent might say to a child about the uneaten food on their plate. Imagine seeing all your favorite foods prepared on the table before you. You put some of every-thing on your plate but you are unable to eat it all.

"Eat all of your food, there are kids starving in Africa". Something a parent or an older sibling might say.

"It's about time for the cow to 'come-in'." It is time for the cow to deliver her calf or give birth.

"I can look through muddy water and spot dry land". Some hyperbole by someone making a claim relative to their visual acuity.

"Leventy-leven dozen". A non-number that implies a significant quantity.

"Umpteen" or "Umpteenth". Cousin to Leventy-leven dozen.

A way to convey that a relatively large number of people were at a given place/event, would be to say that "Everybody and their mama" was there.

"I reckon I better C-O-W". The person uttering these words was declaring that it is time to go or to leave. This was generally a conversation between old people, and kind of a play on perhaps a lack of formal education.

"You don't have a pot to piss in nor a window to throw it out of." Generally meaning, you got squat; to be without resources. A general reference to a person or family on the low end or bottom of the economic ladder.

"Piss or get off the pot" would be said to an indecisive person, imploring them to 'make a decision' one way or the other, particularly if the person was impeding others. A similar, but kinder expression is, "Fish or cut bait".

"Who died and left you in charge?" Asked of someone acting or behaving in a way as if they had some kind of authority when none actually existed.

"Acting like a big hen's poot" – acting or behaving with some air of superiority or in a better light then someone else. Poot is a synonym for fart (passing gas, flatulence).

Our parents would send us on an errand. Invariably they would say "and don't tarry", meaning do not take longer than necessary or required.

"Cc city ss state, a letter like this don't need no date." Something a person might put on a letter to someone for whom they had feelings; love/infatuation. It was one of those corny thing adolescents wrote back in the day.

"Clean as a rat's turd in a dresser draw". A low-brow but sincere compliment bestowed on someone that was dressed nicely; or, a sarcastic-like compliment to some- one who thought they were dressed nicely. Presumably a rat's turd in a dresser draw was better off than the same turd in the stable. Turd refers to solid feces.

Mothers, an older sibling, or another person might threaten to "slap you into next week" or "slap the black of ya". Generally, something someone might say to you in anger; especially if you were getting on their nerves.

Someone might jokingly threaten to "beat you like you stole a government mule". This expression was modernized to "beat you like you stole a government check".

"Sticks and stones may break my bones but words never hurt me."

"I made you look, you dirty crook, you stole your mama's pocketbook."

Although not specifically related to April Fool's Day, this might be said by the person that had jokingly made someone look for something that was not really there.

Acting "mannish". Typically, a boy acting in a sexual suggestive manner, often beyond what might be expected for his age.

"Fast". Analogous to "Mannish" but for a girl acting in a sexual suggestive manner, often beyond what might be expected for her age.

"Smells herself", "smelling herself". Refers to a girl acting too grown for her age; suggesting that a girl has begun to smell her womanhood. To be fair, it probably was applied to boys as well.

If someone tries to get your attention by saying "Hey!". You might reply by saying "Horses eat hay!". Generally meaning, do not address me that way.

"The rabbit died". The person of concern was pregnant.

"The stork is coming". A way of explaining to a young child that a baby will arrive soon without going into details about child-birth.

If a female was animated in displaying the fact that she was upset about something, someone might say that she is acting like she is going to have "A hay-baby with a green-grass neck".

The "Three S's". Shit, shower, and shave. Popularized by military personnel before it became a more common expression. Similar to "Three hots and a cot", also a popular military expression before it came to be identified with incarcerated persons. A reference to three meals each day and a place to sleep.

"Throw water up and run under it" means that someone was going to take the briefest possible shower.

"Timbuktu". A place where someone might threaten to knock you, or a place someone might ask you to go (as in get lost). Probably not all persons using the expression knew that Timbuktu is an actual place, but probably understood the implication to get far away.

"A hard head makes for a soft behind." The person with a hard head misbehaves (likely repeatedly). Therefore, that person almost certainly got spankings or whippings. The spankings or whippings on the behind would in theory 'soften' it up, much like tenderizing a steak with that mallet-like utensil.

"If the good Lord is willing and the creek don't rise." Like many expressions it's a play on words. Someone might ask, 'are you coming to my house tomorrow?' No, if the creek (that I must cross) rises. Yes, if the Lord is willing. Of course, if the Lord is willing or unwilling, it does not matter whether the creek rises or not. A similar expression is "If the Lord say the same".

"Going to see the turtle take water, or take to water." A quick response when someone asks "where are you going?" but you have no intention of telling them.

"Burning daylight." What you might say to someone who is still in the bed (sleep) when they should already be up and about a task. It could also be said to or of someone that is not making efficient use of time and thus wasting the light of day.

A "Fork in the road" – What this means probably depends on who you ask. Some would think of it like the letter "T" or the letter "Y". If you are traveling on the vertical part, you would eventually come to a fork in the road; meaning you would have to decide whether to go to the right or the left. Someone else might think of it more like a plus sign (+). In this case, in addition to right or left, you could decide to go straight ahead. In any case the moral of the expression is that a decision has to be made. Then there is the philosophical "Fork in the road".

"The bottom." Land, a field, or a dwelling area that was more or less surrounded by hills or higher terrain.

"Cross my heart and hope to die". A kinder and gentler way of swearing.

"Pulling my leg" – telling someone a story that they should sooner or later see through. They might respond "you're pulling my leg", or otherwise you let them off the hook by saying to them "I'm pulling your leg".

Being called "country". A reference to someone that typically lives or lived in a rural area. Their behavior or speech would likely differ from persons raised in an urban environment.

"The blacker the berry the sweeter the juice". This was generally a response to someone speaking negatively of a person's darker skin complexion.

"What's good for the goose is good for the gander" means what's good for a male is also good for a female. This could apply in a variety of scenarios but more often was a reference to cheating (stepping out on one's significant other).

"Knee baby". This baby or child was the second youngest if there is three or more siblings.

References to father and mother: Father, dad, daddy, papa, pops; Mother, mommy, mama, mom, muh, muh dear

"Cuttin, or cut'n" – ways of referring to cousins or relatives.

"Son son so". An expression to avoid naming a person. Maybe you cannot recall the name, or a hypothetical person.

"Cooking with gas". A widely used expression to imply what was wrong had been righted, what was bad has been made good, what was inefficient has been made efficient, etc. Back in the day cooking was done using a wood burning stove. The heating of the home was done using a wood burning heater. The cooking/heating was so much quicker and easier when the wood burning stove/ heater was replaced with a gas stove. Therefore, it was an improvement or things were better when "cooking" and heating with gas.

"Fair to middlin". Someone would ask another person, "how are you doing?" The person might respond fair to middlin'. Roughly translated, I am just better than doing bad, or middlin, in the middle of that same imaginary scale.

"Cut a rug" – the ability to 'dance'. Often a reference to a more senior or 'old' person, and/or a pronouncement made by a more senior person.

"Put your foot in it". An expression generally used in reference to cooking. If the food is very tasty, a compliment would be to say, honey, "You put your foot in those greens".

"Slim pickings" is the opposite of plentiful, e.g. few or little. It could refer to the quantity, the quality, or the limitation in the choices. "slim-to-none" is an extension of that expression, inclusive of zero or none.

"Don't throw the baby out with the bath water" refers to when multiple individuals would sequentially and perhaps chronologically take a bath in the same bath water. One could hypothesize that the baby would be last to take its bath and could accidently be discarded with the dirty water. Of course, its actual usage is more generalized. For example, do not discard something in its entirety if there are useful parts.

"If the shoe fits", or "If the shoe fits, wear it". Means that if a less than complimentary statement could apply to you, than it applies to you, although you may or may not have been the target of the statement.

"The early bird gets the worm". Some worms come out at night (e.g. Nightcrawlers). The birds that hunt earliest in the morning will get to eat the (most) worms. By extension, the person that is early/timely gets/has the advantage.

"Sowing wild oats". Generally, refers to a young unmarried man and his pre-marital sexual experimentation.

"Spanking brand new". A really new item or purchase, not just 'new to you' but really new.

"Is a pig pork?" A retort to a question, such that you want to ensure that your "yes" answer comes through.

"You cannot make a silk purse out of a sow's ear."

"There is more than one way to skin a cat". There is more than one way to complete a task.

"Mama said there would be days like this."

"You don't miss you water until your well runs dry."

"You can take a horse to water but you cannot make it drink"

"Putting the cart before the horse" implies the order is reversed and ill-advised.

"Why buy the whole cow when you can get the milk for free." This generally meant, why make a great commitment when the lesser one provides the desired outcome? This expression often referred to marital intimacy versus intimacy without the benefit of marriage.

"Not worth a hill of beans" or "Not worth a hill of rotten beans". Someone or something is presumed to be worthless.

"Time will tell."

"If you can't say something good about a person, then don't say anything."

"Mama's baby, papa's maybe."

"Guess I will (or we will) head on back to the po house."

"Between me, you, and the lamp post." An introductory phrase that says whatever follows is being told to you in confidence (perhaps a secret).

"Knee-high to a duck." Generally referring to when the person, that is the object of the statement, was a kid and thusly short in stature.

"Your (our) neck of the wood" generally refers to where someone lives.

"Wake up dead" is left to one's imagination. Possibly a paranormal experience where the spirit leaves the body recognizing that the body is dead

"It is better to keep your mouth shut and let people think that you are a fool, then to open your mouth and remove all doubt."

"A day late and a dollar short."

"Don't let the door knob hit ya, where the good Lord split ya (*variation*: "Don't let the door knob hit ya, where the dog should have bit ya")

"Shitting and stepping back in it" – a bad situation is being made worse.

"Going to hell in a hand basket" – a situation, or one's outlook is rapidly getting worse

"Idle hands are the devil's workshop"

"Kick(ed) the bucket" refers to someone's passing

"Henpecked" a way of labeling a person who repeatedly yields to someone for whom the person has feelings.

"Barnyard pimp" – most generically speaking, a chicken. Perhaps the ones that strutted around the yard, e.g. a rooster.

"When the chickens come home to roost" – something was done seemingly without consequence, but sooner or later consequences become apparent.

"Scarce as hen's teeth" – when one is short of something or totally without, they may utter this phrase as chickens do not have teeth.

"By the skin of my teeth" usually denotes how close one came to something that would have been detrimental except for the narrow escape.

"You cannot walk and chew gum at the same time" – basically telling someone that they cannot do two or more things simultaneously.

"I haven't seen you in a month of Sundays". Haven't seen you over a significant span of time.

"Blind in one eye and cannot see out of the other."

"Use your head for more than a hat rack."

When someone finished doing a lady's hair, the lady would say "Mo hair" or "More hair" instead of saying thank you.

"My name is Puddin' Tame, ask me again and I'm tell you the same." This would be in response to someone asking your name, and you're not inclined to tell them.

"Six in one hand, a half-dozen in the other."

"If it had been a snake, it would have bit you" means something you were looking for turned out to be essentially in plain sight, often in close proximity to you.

"Shake what your mama gave you." Typically, a crude pronouncement to someone dancing.

Expressions that imply that someone was moving very fast or speedily; "hauling ass", "like a bat out of hell", and "like a scalded dog".

There were/are many expressions involving "Tom, Dick, and Harry". The expressions generally started with the word "Don't". For example, don't fall in love with every Tom, Dick, and Harry you see.

If someone calls you 'chicken' after having dared you to do something (particularly something with an element of danger), it would be acceptable to reply "It is better to be a live chicken than a dead duck."

CHAPTER SEVENTEEN

Unconventional Customs

T hese are things we did for various reason, or possibly for no reason at all. One probably should not over think them. Caution! Do not try some of these at home as it could lead to injury; or you just looking stupid. Speaking 'Pig Latin'. This pseudo-language would be used by two or more individuals to have private communication in the presence of others.

Striking a wooden match while holding it close to the head and raking it along the thigh with a quick stroke (the person's leg would typically be raised so that the thigh would be parallel to the floor/ground). This worked best when wearing denim or cotton pants. This practice had a touch of machismo about it.

Sharing a stick of gum. Someone would share a stick of chewing gum with two or more kids. The kids would have to try and divide the stick of gum equally. The rule was the person doing the dividing got the smallest piece.

Temporarily stored chewed gum by placing it behind the ear, e.g. while sharing a bite of someone's sandwich; after which, one would retrieve and resume chewing the gum.

We loved to have mom clean out our ears using a hair clamp. Not sure we were all that concern about hygiene but rather just enjoyed the personal care of a mom's touch.

Joyfully spanking someone to celebrate their birthday; number of licks equated to the person's age. The cutoff age for this was somewhere around ten to twelve years of age.

Plant a 'big loogy' or spit on a baby's bottom to aid in the cleanup process when changing a soiled diaper.

Collect Blue Horse (points), and Dum Dum candy wrappers to be redeemed for novelty prizes. The Blue Horse typically came inside a pack of lined school paper. We would also order small toys and other items from novelty catalogs.

Turning eyelids inside out, rolling or making waves with the stomach, making eye balls look hard to the nose simultaneously. These antics were generally done to entertain or frighten young children.

Even back in the day some folks had one or more (white or yellow) gold teeth, not the mouth-full that some celebrities have today. As adolescents or teenagers, we could only afford to simulate gold teeth. We would take the wrapping paper from a stick of gum or some candy and cover a tooth so it looked like we had a gold tooth. Then we would smile from ear to ear.

Bronze baby shoes – When a baby outgrew those white hard-sole shoes, the parents would have the shoes bronzed. Those same shoe that, at times, had the jingle bell attached to them, presumably to help keep track of the little ankle-biter. The bronzed shoes would become the centerpiece of an ornamental arrangement that included a photo of the baby. The arrangement would be prominently displayed in the room where guests would be received.

Skimmed grease off the top of cold dish water. The grease would be used like lotions and moisturizers. This was done when lotion and the usual alternative, petroleum jelly, had been used up.

Stomping Things – During elementary and middle school years we used to love stomping the pint-size milk cartons. We received free milk on a daily basis in a half-pint carton. We'd stomp the empty carton and they would pop making a loud noise. We had a similar practice with a plant we referred to as Maypops. They would also make a popping sound. Note that the insides of the maypops could be eaten when caught at the appropriate ripened stage.

Making a 'smoking pipe' from an unnamed/wild plant/ stalk that had a bulb in the middle of the stalk.

Making cigarettes by pouring purchased tobacco into 'rolling paper'.

Smoking rabbit tobacco. Something adolescents did. This supposed tobacco came from a plant that grew wild. Children would make rolled 'cigarettes' and try smoking, perhaps for the first time.

Eating dirt. This was not just any dirt! The dirt was like pornography; we cannot accurately describe it but we knew it when we saw it. The dirt would typically be on a bank/hill, e.g. where a road had been cut through a high elevation. One would break of a piece of the dirt much like a person breaking of a piece of chewing tobacco.

Licking the spoon and the bowl used to make a cake. If you could not get your face sufficiently inside the bowl, you could collect the batter remnant on your hand. At some point the fear of salmonella was put into us and we stopped this practice. One cannot make a cake without breaking some eggs. We are confident that the practice has not ceased completely.

Emptying a vending machine-size bag of salted peanuts into a bottle of soda. The only logic was that it tasted good. However, there was the practical aspect of not having to hold the soda in one hand and the peanuts in the other.

Consuming honeysucker nectar. It tastes sweet, but there is such a small quantity, we are not sure why we bothered.

Males removed headgear when entering a building, especially houses of worship.

Put both hands together to form a cup in order to scoop up water to drink (from a source of water outside of the house).

Cupping one hand into the other, then bring the thumbs together to make a "human-hand horn". By flapping the outer hand, the sound would vary.

Siphoning gasoline from a vehicle of some kind using a rubber hose; typically, in order to put gas into a small engine, e.g. lawn mower, chain saw, etc. There was a high degree of certainty of you getting a mouth full of gas before mastering the process. While we never did it, there were rumors that one or more less than stellar citizens would occasionally siphon gasoline from school buses. The buses were typically parked at the driver's house overnight.

Simultaneously elevate a butt cheek while slapping it with the open hand. This was an invitation to the person, with whom you were having a disagreement, to kiss your butt. This was most dramatic when done as you walked away.

CHAPTER EIGHTEEN

Miscellaneous

The Box Project and Mrs. Kisfe

O ur Mission: To encourage and enrich the lives of families and individuals living in rural poverty by establishing meaningful relationships, promoting education, and offering material aid." (boxproject.org)

On occasions our parents would receive packages in the mail. The packages would be filled with household items, food items and treats. As children we probably did not know, and maybe did not care, where the packages came from. We were just happy that they came. The packages were particularly welcomed during the Christmas holiday. It seems like there would always be a box of "Indian River" oranges from Florida. Children in a given age range would get inexpensive but nice gift items. Some gift were more memorable than others; perhaps they were durable as well. There were a couple of ponies, about the size of a loaf of bread. They had more lives than the proverbial cat. Eventually we came to know that our angel's name was Mrs. Kisfe. She lived in up-state Maine. Many of the siblings began our own personal communication with Mrs. Kisfe as we became of age and throughout adulthood until she passed. She was great at responding to our letters. We counted her in the number as we figured out how many class pictures and especially graduation pictures to have printed. Not only did she remember our birthdays, but she began to do the same for our children. She continued to communicate with our family beyond her participation in the program. She provided monetary gifts, clothing, and holiday baskets of various fruits. Several siblings got to visit with her in person. The first visit was made by three adult siblings. The second trip include those same siblings, their spouses, and their children. It was a family reunion of sort. She had many of the pictures we sent her displayed throughout her home. She was an angel on this side of Jordan. Surely, she has wings now.

Mail Delivery

The 'mailman' used his own vehicle to deliver the mail. He did not wear a uniform, nor did his vehicle have any special markings. We came to recognize the vehicle when it was coming. The mail was delivered to a free-standing mailbox at the road; the same way it is currently delivered. However, at times the box was some distance away as part of a cluster of boxes. Presumably this allowed the mailman to minimize the number of stops and the distance driven. Mail was delivered via "General delivery", "Rural free delivery (RFD)", eventually 'Route x Box y' addresses, where x and y are numerals. Somehow, this related to the fact that we lived far away from the city, on mostly unpaved roads. As part of the 9/11/2001 changes, those same addresses are more like xxx County Road yyy, or xxx Highway yyy for those living on a highway. We always found it interesting that back in the day, if you wanted a government document sent to you, you had to send a stamped, self-addressed envelope to some address in Pueblo, Colorado. What was up with that?

CHAPTER NINETEEN

The Exodus

B ecause of the lack of opportunities and other ineq-
uities, many young men left the community and
even the state. Many, if not most of them, headed north to
places like Chicago, Milwaukee, Flint and other industri-
alized cities. Some of the ones that had gone to college,
left after graduation for graduate schools in other states.
Schools out of state presented more opportunities for
internships, post graduate work, and were often in
region with permanent, well-paying jobs. Similar scenarios played out as well for young men that went into
the military. Often when a sibling or cousin established
residency out of state or in other parts of the state, it
became a draw and an opportunity for others to relo-
cate to that state or area. Over the course of a couple

of decades, most of our siblings ended up in Illinois, Georgia, Maryland, Tennessee and other cities within the state but several hours of driving from the homestead. A small minority of siblings settled and remained in our home county and city. We understand that similar migration occurred as individuals or families moved from the Carolinas to New York, Florida, the District of Columbia and elsewhere. Many of the individuals and families that left home in search of better opportunities, harbored notions of returning once opportunities became available in and around our home town. However, those opportunities were slow in coming, if they came at all. Therefore, the return has been slow at best. The typical return has been persons that have retired and yearned for the slower pace and/or the warmer winters enjoyed 'back home'. If someone found love and married someone in the place they migrated to, the spouse is less likely to want to be uprooted to take up residency in what seems to them to be a foreign land. Forget it, particularly if there are grandchildren involved (word to the wise). On the up side, the migration contributed to geographical and cultural exposure as we traveled to visit each other during special events such as vacations, marriage ceremonies, graduations and family reunions. If everyone stayed put, our world would likely have been much smaller. Thank God for a network of interstate highways and airports that enabled travel by those so inclined, including making frequent trips back home to see love ones, especially aging seniors that had been prominent in our lives.

CHAPTER TWENTY

Family Gatherings

Reunions

The patriarchs and matriarchs of the family instilled in us the importance of family. They would show this by bring us together over food, good conversations, games, church, etc. It was just something we did periodically. Somewhere along the way someone began referring to the informal get-togethers as a family reunion. The earliest reunions we attended were not really reunions in the modern sense. They were not planned as large extended family or community events. At some point we somehow began assembling at Aunt Maria's house annually. I suppose she told her siblings and they in turn told their grown and minor children. Of course, it is equally conceivable that Aunt Maria's siblings, and/or their spouses, conspired behind her back and somehow convinced her to actually suggest the event. Who would turn down Maria? She was the oldest of our father's sisters and became our self-appointed surrogate after our mother's passing. She loved to cook and entertain guests, and we loved to eat what she prepared, sometimes even if we were already stuffed as a 3-day burrowed in tick. The gathering was mostly a local event. Relatives did not travel in from far-away places; at least not more than an hour or two away. There were no written invitations, no collection of funds. Everyone just showed up. Of course, grownups knew to bring one or more dishes, otherwise by default you volunteer to work in the crowded, noisy, hot kitchen to ensure that enough food was prepared. Presumably there was some coordination behind the scene. There seem to be some of everyone's favorite food. After having the main course (and seconds), the women gathered to chat while the men went outside to smoke, dipped snuff, and tell tall tales. The children chased the ever-present fowls (turkey and geese); raced to and cleared the plum trees, etc. Then came the time for making ice cream. There was the adage that there is always room for ice cream. One or more grownups would handle the recipe and ingredients while the children took turns providing the horsepower necessary to turn the crank of the ice cream maker. You could have any flavor of ice cream you wanted as long as it was whitish in color and tasted like vanilla. Those were the days! As our generation of siblings matured; some got married, had children of their own, some went off to college, the military, or simply move away to distant places. As the generation of our parents began to transition to a better home beyond these celestial shores, the gatherings became fewer and further apart. At some point the gatherings evolved or devolved into a family gathering centered around our father and our siblings. By this time only one of our father's siblings remained. We even started calling it the Branch-Fullilove Family Gathering. Fullilove being our mother's last name from her first marriage and thereby the last name of the eldest three siblings. By now a number of siblings had made their home in other states. So, the gatherings began to take on a nomadic aspect which persist to this day. The Family Gatherings began to move around to other cities within the state and to other states. The new approach gave many family members a reason to travel to places they likely would not have gone otherwise. Since the show was taken on the road, so to speak, the potluck food caravan was no longer viable. Now the host family had to plan the food, research hotels, play shuttle drivers, and scout out tourist sites and other interesting places to visit. The assessment of fees to each family based on the size of the family became the norm. That process continues today, notwithstanding the breaks in 2020 through 2022 due to the coronavirus pandemic. This annual gathering is centered around our father's side of the family. With eight girls and seven boys (two now deceased), the siblings and their off-springs, form the core of the reunions, pretty much all of the attendees when the gathering is held outside of the state of Mississippi. A couple of cousins often travel to be with us. The weekend-long event typically started with folks arriving Friday and attending a casual event that evening that often involves a fish-fry. Quite often we would not have seen each other since the previous year's reunion. Saturday would be the day for a brief meeting attended by siblings, spouses, and adult children; followed by a picnic. We try to attend church service Sunday morning, together if practical, then have a meal together before breaking camp. Before departing, we decide where we plan to get together the following year.

Graduations

As the brothers' and sisters' children began to age, the kids' high school graduations became the events to gather around. Wanting to be supportive of these graduates, families started traveling to high school graduations. Many of these graduations were outside of the state of Mississippi as well. In addition to the usual elements of a family reunion, the host family also had to contemplate the logistics of a significant number of family members wanting to attending the high school graduation. Thirty nieces and nephews have graduated. Fortunately, some of them were in the same class and/or the same location. If you get enough of family in one location, even for a day, then it makes for a family gathering. The Mississippi graduations occurred in early May; typically closed to Mother's Day. Unlike our smaller

Mississippi high school, graduations in larger metropolitan area happened closer to (sometime after) Memorial Day and were not constrained to the weekend. On the other hand, who has a family gathering in the middle of the week? If someone wanted to make a vacation of it, they might catch a weekday graduation. The family gathering would be the weekend before or after; whichever made the most sense; and if the graduation occurred close to a special day (e.g. Memorial Day), all the better! The family would get to see each other, hang out, and the graduate would get the honor, and gifts, befitting their achievement. Graduation was another opportunity for the graduates and family members attending the ceremony to dress up in one's Sunday best. This meant, males wore a suit or similar ensemble. The female wore spring/summer dresses. These were also opportunities to wear those Easter outfits again.

Weddings

Often, the wedding for the older siblings was a matter of a visit to the local Justice of the Peace. No one ran off to Las Vega in order to tie the knot. The sentiment of love was present all the same. Over time the ceremonies grew grander in term of size and complexity. Most were officiated by an ordained minister and took place in a church; there were no outdoor weddings. The essence of the ceremonies continued to be very traditional; no unique vows, or jumping over brooms, etc. All siblings are or were married at one time or another. A couple of marriages ended by virtue of divorce and several ended by virtue of the death of our sibling or his/her spouse. Most of our siblings met and married sweethearts from the larger local community. A few met their mate in college, and others after having established domicile in other states. This meant that family had to take to the road to participate in those nuptials. Most weddings included a reception. Wedding receptions are generally a family gathering of sort with the addition of a whole other family plus friends and acquaintances of the bride and groom. It is easy to imagine that this would be the most photographed of gatherings.

Funerals

We have had the misfortune to lose two siblings; in our mind, way before their time (late 50, early 60). One lived and died in our native county, the other some 1000 miles away. Of course, we were sad having to attend their funerals and the funerals of an untold number of friends and relatives, including our father in 2002 at the age of 89. Our mother passed some 28 years prior. The community had a tradition of taking a food dish to the house of the recently bereaved. Planning and sitting through funerals are always solemn occasions. Often the grave site was in walking distance of the church. After the service there would be a processional to the grave site. Early on the graves were dug by men using shovels. Almost all funeral services were held inside of a church. Once funeral homes added sufficiently sized chapels, some services are held at the funeral home. Funerals were traditionally held on Saturday or Sunday, presumably to avoid interrupting the work-week. After the final rites at graveside, the family would depart, but a number of males would be asked to remain in order to cover the grave. Generally, after the internment activities, a repast takes place. This is essentially a gathering of family, friends, and acquaintances. However, as one would expect, in this case the atmosphere is less festive. Much has changed over the years, yet much remains the same.

The practice of dressing up for special events is slowly falling by the way side, especially among the younger generations. More revealing clothing, casual clothing (e.g. jeans, sneakers), funky colors, etc. are all finding a level of acceptance or tolerance these days.

CHAPTER TWENTY-ONE

Final Thoughts

M any families, especially black families that lived off the land, had a hard time making ends meet. Therefore, getting ahead often seemed like a pipe dream. However, they never lost hope that their children would not suffer the same fate. Parents, no doubt intentionally, did not go around crying "woe is me". Children were aware that some folks, particularly white folks, appeared to be better off than their family. While we may have grown up financially challenged, we were not lacking in spirit. A caring community instilled in its children, that, where we were in life, at the time, would not define where we would be in the future. There was very little criminal activity to speak of. Drug use was something heard about on the news, at least until marijuana became readily available. Farming slowly but surely became a more upscale operation. Small farmers became even less competitive. To put things in perspective, we were not deprived like our fore-parents that came to this country as slaves or were born into slavery. Then there were the post emancipation and Jim Crow years. We are children of the Jim Crow and the Civil Rights eras. We could not envision how we could do justice to a discussion of those perilous times within the confine of these pages. Thanks to hard work, our parents were better off than their parents, and we are better off than our parents, at least economically. Some have argued against that over simplification; and to a degree, they are correct. We have made many strides. We like to think that we triumphed against the odds. This book is a minor attempt to fill the gap that once occurred naturally through the tradition of passing down family history through oral story telling. It is probably too much to expect that each reader will seek to reverse the loss of the oral tradition. If one family is moved to sit around the dinner table, or on the back porch (now screened in) and rekindle those conversations, then the universe will be pleased. Let it begin with me! Thank you, Lord, for our tests and our testimonies!

The End

www.ingramcontent.com/pod-product-compliance
Lightning Source LLC
Chambersburg PA
CBHW070723130626
46553CB00005B/2125